working with
colour healing

working with
colour healing

how to use colour to heal your
body and enhance your life

Jane Struthers

A GODSFIELD BOOK

To Bill

An Hachette Livre UK Company
www.hachettelivre.co.uk

First published in Great Britain in 2008 by
Godsfield Press, a division of Octopus Publishing Group Ltd
2–4 Heron Quays, London E14 4JP
www.octopusbooks.co.uk

Distributed in the United States and Canada by
Sterling Publishing Co., Inc.
387 Park Avenue South, New York, NY 10016-8810

ISBN 978-1-841-81331-8

A CIP catalogue record of this book is available from the British Library.

Printed and bound in China

2 4 6 8 10 9 7 5 3 1

Disclaimer
The information given in this book is not intended to act as a substitute for
medical treatment, nor can it be used for diagnosis. Colour healing is a powerful
therapy and can be open to misunderstanding or abuse. If you are in any doubt
about its use, you should consult a qualified colour healing practitioner.

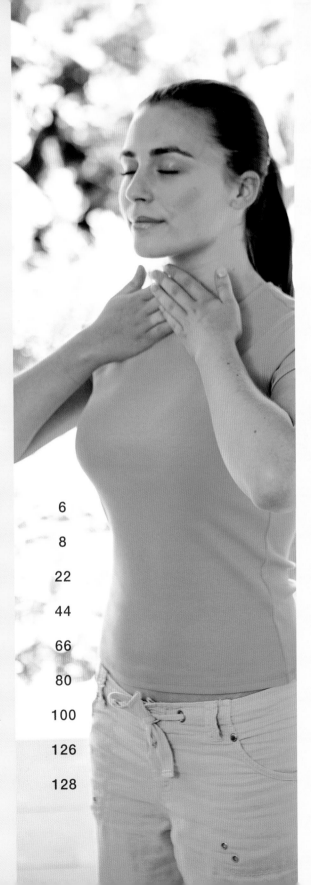

contents

INTRODUCTION

We are surrounded by colour. We can't be separated from it. It is in the air around us and it continually has an impact on us, even if we aren't aware of it. Colour is a form of energy and it is connected to us through our auras – the electromagnetic field that surrounds our bodies. The clothes we wear, the food we eat, the colours in our homes ... they all affect us, whether we know it or not.

You don't have to be able to see colour for it to affect and benefit you. That is why blind people are affected by colour in many of the same ways as sighted people. Our bodies react to the colour rays and use them in whichever way they are needed.

living with colour

This book introduces you to the power of colour in your life. It will help you to become more aware of the effect that different colours have on you, and teach you how to use colour to improve your day-to-day life, brighten your mood, increase your creativity, help you to sleep peacefully, create a happy home and connect with the spiritual realms. If you wish, you can also use colour to work with the angels. As you start to become more aware of the benefits of the different colours, your life will gain more meaning, especially at a deep, spiritual level. You will also learn how to use colour healing to improve your health.

what is colour healing?

Colour healing is the technique of treating illness through the application of colour. This involves a wide range of therapies, from complicated techniques that are best left to qualified practitioners to very simple treatments that can easily be used at home.

The techniques in this book include colour healing with the help of crystals, diet, clothing, contact healing, coloured silks, solarized or colour-impregnated water, colour meditations, colour visualizations, healing gardens and the colours in our homes.

Each colour healing technique uses the vibrational energy of colour to treat ailments and illnesses and to create balance and harmony within the body.

when should you use colour healing?

Colour healing helps to treat disease but it can also help to prevent it. You can use it to keep your body healthy, and to correct any imbalances within your body before they cause physical or mental problems. You can do this simply by being more aware of the colours of the food you eat, the colours in your home and the colours of your clothes. You can also become more aware of how you feel – mentally, physically, emotionally and spiritually. This will enable you to notice when something doesn't feel right and you can treat it accordingly, using colour.

However, colour healing should never be used as a substitute for medical care. If you're worried about your health, you should seek professional medical advice immediately. Once you've sought help, you can use colour healing to augment any treatment you're given or to help alleviate any medical condition that you have. For instance, applying a cold compress of violet-impregnated water could help to soothe the discomfort of a painful arthritic joint.

You can mix colour healing with any other complementary therapy, too. However, whether you're using it in conjunction with conventional or complementary medicine, or on its own, you should always treat colour healing with respect. Colour has powerful effects on the human body.

Jane Struthers

THE SCIENCE OF COLOUR

Colour is everywhere – the blue of the sky, the green of the grass, the pink of your dog's nose, the yellow of the bananas in your fruit bowl. The world resonates to the vibrations emitted by the colours around us, and we are affected by them in many different ways. Yet we are often unaware of the power of colour until we awaken to it and start to actively use it in our lives. Once that happens, our relationship with colour is never the same again, and we can begin to use colour to bring ourselves many benefits on spiritual, emotional, mental and physical levels.

This chapter introduces you to the power of colour. It describes the science of colour, including what it is and how we are able to see it, and the relationship of the colours to one another. It also gives some of the history of colour healing, and a few of the forms it can take. Other forms of colour healing will be explored in detail throughout the rest of the book. This chapter also discusses the seven colour rays and the angels that are associated with them.

what is colour?

Have you ever wondered what colour actually is? Until you have a grasp of the nature of colour you won't be able to understand why colour healing has such power.

the ancient Greeks

Scientists and philosophers have ruminated on the nature of colour for thousands of years. The Greek philosophers were particularly interested in colour as it was an important part of their healing repertoire. Pythagoras (c. 580–500 BCE) believed that objects emit particles, which enable us to see them. Aristotle (384–322 BCE) took this theory one step further and suggested that light travels in waves. He also theorized that the colours we see are linked to one of the four elements – fire, earth, air and water – from the doctrine of humours (see page 15), and gave a metaphysical slant to the science of colour.

The work of Sir Isaac Newton, the natural philosopher and mathematician, had a radical impact on the science of colour.

the theory of wavelengths

Sir Isaac Newton (1642–1727) divided the light spectrum into seven colours (see pages 12–13). He theorized that light consists of waves, and that each colour of the spectrum operates at a different wavelength.

Quantum physics, whose main exponents included Max Planck (1858–1947) and Albert Einstein (1879–1955), concluded that the theories of Aristotle and Pythagoras were partly correct. Experiments found that the colours of the spectrum consist of small parcels of energy, known as photons, and that these move in waves. Where the wavelength is short, the photons are compressed and there is a lot of energy. This wavelength has a high frequency (the number of times the wave oscillates in one second). Where the wavelength is long, the photons are further apart and there is correspondingly less energy. This wavelength has a low frequency.

The beautiful colours in a rainbow, which always appears opposite the Sun, are caused by the refraction and internal reflection of light in raindrops.

colour and the electromagnetic spectrum

The colours that we can see are part of the electromagnetic spectrum, which is the name given to all the energy in the known universe. The electromagnetic spectrum is measured in nanometres – millionths of one millimetre. One end consists of radio waves – long wavelengths, low frequency and the least amount of energy – and the other end consists of cosmic waves – short wavelengths, high frequency and a great deal of energy. We cannot see most of the energy on the electromagnetic spectrum, but we can see colours, which are currently believed to fall in the middle of this spectrum.

Red has the longest wavelength, the lowest frequency and the least energy. Beyond it are infrared rays and radio waves, which we can't see. Violet, at the other end of the colour spectrum, has the shortest wavelength, the highest frequency and the greatest amount of energy. Beyond violet are ultraviolet light, X-rays, gamma rays and cosmic rays.

The colours that are visible to the naked eye occupy a relatively small area in the middle of the electro-magnetic spectrum.

Because these have the highest levels of energy, they have the potential to cause the most damage to living organisms.

Even if you can't grasp quantum physics, you only need to remember one important fact about the science of colour and that is, colour is energy. It penetrates the cells in our bodies just as easily as the X-rays further up the electromagnetic spectrum.

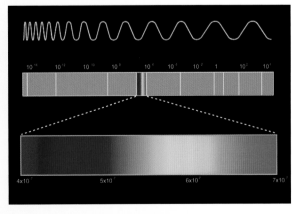

the colour wheel

One of the easiest ways to understand the relationship between colours is to view them in the form of a colour wheel. This shows the neighbouring colours in the spectrum (known as analogous colours) and also reveals the colours that oppose each other (known as complementary colours).

The colour wheel is especially useful to painters, whose work is highly influenced by the relationships between colours, and also to practitioners of colour healing because they work extensively with complementary colours. However, it's important to remember that pigments in paint have different properties from coloured lights.

Goethe divided colour into two psychological groups. The plus group (which promotes cheerfulness) consists of red, orange and yellow, and the negative group (which causes unsettled emotions) consists of green, blue and violet.

how many colours are there?

Opinion is divided about the number of colours in the spectrum. It seems that colour is a very subjective topic – we see what we want to see. The British scientist Sir Isaac Newton discovered the colour spectrum by shining a white light through a prism; the light refracted into distinct bands of colour. Newton identified these as red, orange, yellow, green, blue, indigo and violet. However, there is a theory that he didn't see seven bands of colour at all: he saw six (red, orange, yellow, green, blue and violet). He added indigo to turn these into seven colours, because seven is a mystical number and this suited his view of the cosmos. When the German poet and painter J.W. von Goethe (1749–1832) conducted his own research into colour, he detected six colours of the spectrum: red, orange, yellow, green, blue and violet. However, Goethe's reasoning was just as subjective as Newton's: six colours fitted nicely on Goethe's artist's palette.

Since then, colour therapists have perceived eight colours and added turquoise and magenta to Goethe's six colours. This gives the eight-colour wheel used by many colour healers.

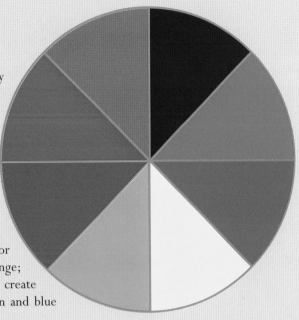

primary and secondary colours

Primary colours are those that can't be made by mixing any other colours together. When using pigments, the primary colours are red, yellow and blue. However, this rule changes for coloured light. Here, the primaries are red, green and blue. If you mix them in equal proportions, the result is white light.

Secondary colours are those made by mixing two primaries together in equal proportion. Once again, these vary according to whether you are using light or pigment. For pigments, red and yellow create orange; yellow and blue create green; and blue and red create violet. For light, red and green make yellow; green and blue make turquoise; and red and blue make magenta.

This is a colour wheel, based on the eight-colour system. Either this, or the seven-colour wheel, can be used for colour healing.

complementary colours

Complementary colours (colours that oppose one another on the colour wheel) are a very important element of colour healing. When viewed as light, complementary colours produce white. In any type of healing, the aim is to create a perfect balance in the body. A colour healer will do this by giving healing with the colour she thinks is most appropriate for her patient and then balance this with the complementary colour. The combination of the two colours provides the most effective form of healing and corrects the imbalance in the patient's body. Treating a patient with only one colour and omitting to balance this with the complementary colour may make the patient's symptoms worse rather than better. In the eight-colour wheel often used for healing, the complementary pairs of colours are red and turquoise, orange and blue, yellow and violet, and green and magenta. These are the colours that are described in this book.

Shining light through a prism is the best way to see how it breaks up into separate colours. You will notice the same effect if sunlight shines on a faceted glass pendant.

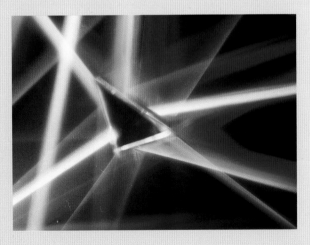

the history of colour healing

Colour healing began thousands of years ago, and it is thought that it was practised in the lost, ancient civilization of Atlantis.

You might imagine that colour healing is a purely New Age therapy but it goes back thousands of years. It seems that we have always used the power of colour to benefit our health.

Atlantis and the ancient Egyptians

It is widely thought that the ancient civilization of Atlantis used colour healing to great effect. Atlanteans built temples that contained special healing rooms with crystal ceilings. When the Sun shone, the crystals refracted the Sun's light on to the patients who received not only the beneficial impact of the colours but also the energies of the crystals. This is theoretical because so far there is no concrete evidence that Atlantis ever existed. The continent is thought to have vanished beneath the sea after its inhabitants abused their extraordinarily advanced technological knowledge and accidentally blew themselves up.

For the ancient Egyptians, colour healing was founded by their god Thoth, and they took it very seriously, creating special healing temples with crystal ceilings. Patients were diagnosed with the colour that they needed, and then treated in the relevant room. Colour was also used for healing. For instance, cataracts of the eye were treated with green obtained from powdered verdigris. The ancient Egyptians also treated illnesses with powdered crystals that were taken internally, rather as gem essences are today. Gemstones were also a classic treatment in ancient India, where each crystal was assigned a particular colour ray.

the ancient Greeks

Colour healing was widely practised in ancient Greece, where it changed from being a metaphysical practice to a scientific one. Sunlight was considered to be a very powerful medicine and Heliopolis was especially celebrated for its healing temples. Heliopolis lent its name to heliotherapy, in which medical treatment is given to patients by practitioners through exposure to the Sun's rays.

The ancient Greeks also believed that the human personality could be divided into four categories, each of which was ruled by a particular colour. Hippocrates (*c*.460–370 BCE) developed this theory, which was still widely followed in medieval Europe. He believed that the human body was composed of four humours and that an imbalance in them led to illness. The four humours were red blood, yellow choler or bile, black choler and white phlegm. Each one corresponded to a particular astrological element, a type of personality and a colour (see chart below).

Avicenna

One of the great colour healers of history was Avicenna (980–1037), the Persian physician. His *Canon of Medicine* described his theories on the action of colour on the human body. For instance, he believed that red increased the circulation of the blood while blue slowed it down, and that yellow helped to reduce pain and inflammation. He treated people's illnesses accordingly, with coloured bandages, flowers and ointments.

Thoth was the Egyptian god of healing, magic and writing. He is thought to have developed colour healing in ancient Egypt.

doctrine of humours

HUMOUR	PERSONALITY	ELEMENT	COLOUR
Red blood	Sanguine (relaxed)	Air	Yellow
Yellow choler	Choleric (irritable)	Fire	Red
Black choler	Melancholic (gloomy)	Water	Blue
White phlegm	Phlegmatic (patient)	Earth	Green

the medieval approach

In the West, medieval architects of churches and cathedrals used the same principles of coloured light as the Atlanteans and ancient Egyptians. Instead of building ceilings made from crystals, they designed intricate stained glass windows. As the sunlight shone through them, the people sitting in the refracted light would receive healing because they would be bathed in the energy of the different colours.

The beautiful colours of stained glass windows are not only decorative. They also perform an important healing function.

Avicenna had been an important practitioner of colour healing (see page 15) and the Swiss physician Paracelsus (1493–1541) was another. He developed many theories and gave colour healing the holistic approach it had lost over the centuries. He believed in treating illness with colour rays, and also with herbs and music. However, his theories were ridiculed and many of his manuscripts were burned.

During the 18th century – the age of enlightenment – science and rational thought took over from metaphysics and spiritual practices; many medieval theories were denounced as mere superstitions, and colour healing was one of them. It wasn't until the 19th century that colour healing resurfaced in a flurry of scientific books written by a succession of authors, culminating in Edwin D. Babbit's *The Principles of Light and Colour*, published in 1878.

the renaissance of colour healing

Babbit's book was revolutionary for its time, although it promulgated many theories that would have been familiar to the ancient Egyptians and Greeks. Babbit discussed the treatment of a variety of ailments with colour, believing that red is a stimulant of the blood, yellow and orange stimulate the nervous system, and blue and violet are calming and anti-inflammatory. Babbit invented special devices for colour healing, including the Thermolune, a cabinet in which the patient sat while being bathed with coloured lights. He also impregnated water with sunlight filtered through coloured lenses – still a common practice today (see pages 82–85). Chromopaths, as colour healers were called, became very popular, although their work was still treated with caution by most of the medical profession.

Steiner and Lüscher

One of the most important 20th-century exponents of colour therapy was Rudolph Steiner (1861–1925). He was greatly inspired by Goethe's work on colour, believing that colour is a living entity and has its own spiritual meaning. He put this theory into practice in the string of schools that he founded, with each area of the school painted a different colour according to its function and the age of the pupils who used it.

The work of Max Lüscher (1923–) on colour was also highly influential. He believed that our colour preferences say a great deal about our psychological make-up as well as our state of health, and he developed the Lüscher Colour Test to prove it.

Edwin D. Babbit was one of the most influential 19th-century practitioners of colour healing. He introduced what he called 'rainbow healing', which used solarized water, in 1878.

Theo Gimbel

In recent years, Theo Gimbel (1920–2004) took colour healing to another level. He developed the technique of spinal diagnosis, in which a chart of a patient's spine is dowsed so that the strength of each vertebra can be ascertained. This is then translated into a colour. Gimbel believed that a healthy spine has eight colours (red, orange, yellow, green, turquoise, blue, violet and magenta) which run in the same repeating sequence up the spine.

complementary and allopathic medicine

Colour healing is still being developed and there are now schools around the world where students can learn to be colour healers. The ever increasing interest in complementary therapies means that colour healing is becoming more widespread. It is also being used in some branches of allopathic medicine. Centuries after its use in the ancient civilizations of the world, the benefits of colour healing are once again being recognized.

angelic realms and colour rays

There is a great deal more to life than what we can detect with our five senses. The air is full of radio waves and the electromagnetic signals from satellites, mobile phones and a host of other technologies. But many other things with a more spiritual connection surround us as well, including angels, our own guardian angels, and the members of the elemental kingdoms such as fairies and elves.

the angelic kingdom

For thousands of years, esoteric writers have described the angelic kingdom. Although many writers have postulated their own theories, on the whole the body of literature about angels is based on the writings of Greek mystic Dionysius the Areopagite (*c.* CE 500), and later on those of St Thomas Aquinas (*c.*1225–74). It's generally believed that the angelic kingdom is divided into nine hierarchies, consisting of three sections or choirs of three orders each, and that each order has a particular function and purpose. The seraphim in the first choir are closest to God. Angels in the third choir work primarily with humans.

Angels are an important part of colour healing because it's believed that each colour ray is ruled by a particular angel. This raises colour healing to an esoteric level, in which you work with angels as well as the colour rays themselves. If you believe in angels, you might like to evoke them when

the angelic kingdom

FIRST CHOIR	SECOND CHOIR	THIRD CHOIR
Seraphim	*Dominions*	*Principalities*
Cherubim	*Virtues*	*Archangels*
Thrones	*Powers*	*Angels*

giving colour healing. If you don't believe in angels, you can simply ignore this facet of colour healing. Working directly with the colours themselves will still be of enormous benefit to you, and it won't be diminished in any way by not working with the angelic realms.

the colours and the angels

Much of what is written about angels is subjective, because it's based on the experience and intuition of the individual writer. Therefore, you'll find that authors sometimes disagree with one another about which angel works with which colour ray. This doesn't mean that one author is wrong and another correct – it simply means that they have different experiences on which they are drawing. Ideally, you should use your own intuition when determining which angel to evoke when working with a particular colour ray. Alternatively, you can simply ask to receive help from whichever angel is appropriate, and know that this has happened.

It is generally believed that archangels work with the seven colour rays. There are millions of archangels in the universe, but very few of them work with humans. Those that do have a colour ray assigned to them, and they work through it in conjunction with their twin flames, which are also known as *archeia*. Archangels aren't in charge of the rays – that is the task of a group of spiritual masters. The Theosophical Movement, which was started by Madame Blavatsky (1831–1891), was instrumental in discovering these connections between the archangels and the seven coloured rays. Theosophy teaches that these rays are guided by a variety of Great Masters, but it is beyond the scope of this book to go into the rulership of them.

It's best to keep your work with the archangels simple at first. You can always discover more about each ray, and the various spiritual masters who work with it, at a later date when you've established a rapport with each of the archangels. Otherwise, immersing yourself too soon in the complicated details of each ray could be confusing and may serve as a distraction rather than give you added focus.

the seven rays

As you read about the rays you will realize that they are not related to the colours of the chakras (see *Colours and the chakras*, pages 44–65). The seven rays belong to an entirely different system.

1 **The first ray** is deep blue, and is associated with Archangel Michael and his archeia Faith. Michael is the angel of courage and protection; if you evoke him he will immediately arrive to protect you with his deep blue cloak and sword. He is the angel to call on if you need instant protection from attack, and also if you want to cut your ties with the past. You may sense his presence around you as flashes of blue light.

2 **The second ray** is yellow-gold, and is associated with Archangel Jophiel and his archeia Christine. They bestow intelligence, illumination and enlightenment. Yellow is the colour of thought, and therefore Jophiel helps in any intellectual endeavour. The yellow of this second ray changes to gold when you begin to attain more wisdom. You can call on Jophiel whenever you need clarification about a situation, you want to adopt a wiser approach to life or you're in need of information.

3 **The third ray** is pink, and is associated with Archangel Chamuel and his archeia Charity. Pink is the colour of unconditional love. Invoke these angels when caught up in a dispute major or minor, and you want to resolve it amicably and for the highest good of all concerned. Projecting pink on to the other people involved and mentally wrapping yourself in pink will evoke Chamuel and lead to a peaceful solution.

4 **The fourth ray** is pure white, and is associated with Archangel Gabriel and his archeia Hope. Gabriel and Hope bestow purity, as well as order, discipline, spirituality and hope. They also provide guidance about your path through life and are therefore the angels to call on when you want to know what to do with your life or you feel lost. They will give you direction and the courage to keep going.

5 The fifth ray is emerald green, and is associated with Archangel Raphael and his archeia Mary, the mother of Jesus. Together they work to bring healing, comfort and intuition. You can call on them when you want to give someone healing, or if you wish to, ask for healing for yourself. They are especially effective when helping with seemingly intractable health problems.

6 The sixth ray is purple and gold, and is associated with Archangel Uriel and his archeia Aurora. They bring peace, spirituality and wisdom. Invoke these angels and concentrate on these colours when you are worried about a difficult situation and you want to understand the motives of the other people involved. Uriel and Aurora will help you to see that there are many sides to any story.

7 The seventh ray is violet, and is associated with Archangel Zadkiel and his archeia Amethyst. They bring emotional freedom that comes from compassion, mercy and tolerance. If you're struggling to find it in your heart to forgive someone, you can ask Zadkiel and Amethyst to help. Mentally surrounding yourself and the other people concerned in violet light will also help to release you from the situation and forgive everyone involved.

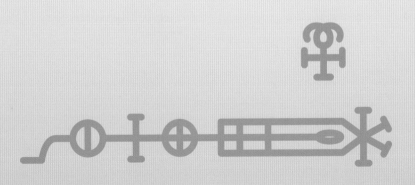

THE POWER OF COLOUR

Each colour has a particular impact on us, even if we aren't aware of it. Blue has a calming and relaxing effect, whereas red is an energizer. Most of us have one or two favourite colours to which we are instinctively drawn, choosing them again and again for our clothes, our homes, our gardens and anything else that gives us pleasure. When asked to explain what draws us to these colours, we may be unable to come up with any coherent explanation.

However, if you want to learn to work with colour, it's important that you understand the impact that each colour has on us, both psychologically and physiologically. This chapter will help you to increase your insight into the power of colour. Colour has profound effects on us at every level.

This chapter will help you to understand why you are drawn to particular colours and what they say about you. It will also teach you the impact that each colour has on us, at a physical, mental, emotional and spiritual level. The colours described consist of the seven so-called natural colours of the spectrum (red, orange, yellow, green, blue, indigo and violet) as well as magenta and turquoise, and black, white, pink and gold.

how colour affects us day-to-day

We are all affected by the colours around us, regardless of whether we can see them. We absorb the energy of each colour in our auras and through our skin. Blind people are therefore affected by colour too. They may not be able to see a particular colour but their bodies will register the impact of its energy at a cellular level. This is how colour healing works – the energy of a particular colour is absorbed into our bodies, affecting all our cells. That is when we are intentionally exposed to a colour for healing purposes. However, this process doesn't switch itself off when we aren't receiving colour healing. It still happens; it's simply that we aren't doing it deliberately.

This means that the colours we surround ourselves with are very important. They have a much bigger impact on us than we might at first think. Once you begin to learn about colour healing, and to practise it, you may want to think again about the colour of your carpets or walls. Equally, you may start to choose objects in colours that you think are appropriate. For instance, you might be drawn to notebooks with yellow covers, because yellow is a colour that stimulates us mentally. You might choose a predominantly blue colour scheme for your bedroom, because now you know that blue is a soothing colour that creates a relaxed atmosphere. The more regularly you work with colour in this way, the more attuned to it you will become and the more sensitive you'll be to the impact that each colour has on you. Don't be surprised if you start to use some colours more sparingly, perhaps because you have become sensitized to them. You may also begin to appreciate other colours to which you've paid little attention in the past.

It pays to choose the colours of our rooms according to the effect that they will have on us. Bedrooms need restful, relaxing colours.

colour marketing

Next time you're out shopping, take a look at the colours around you. This will tell you a lot about the use of colour, and why some companies choose particular colours for their logos. Blue, for instance, conjures up a sense of loyalty and tradition, and therefore dependability. We often speak about someone being 'true blue', meaning they're faithful, so it might be a suitable colour for a financial institution such as a bank. Green is another good colour for a company that deals with money. Green is the colour of growth, and we like to think that our money is going to grow.

marketing yourself

If you have your own company, you need to think about the colours that are associated with it. If your company isn't doing very well, you should consider whether you've chosen a suitable colour for your letterhead or other elements associated with your business. Consider whether the colour sends the right message, and change it if it doesn't.

This woman, attending a business meeting, is sending a subtle message about her trustworthy character by wearing a blue top.

red

Red is the colour of life. It's dynamic, vivid and vibrant. It peps us up, making us feel more energetic and active. In the electromagnetic spectrum, red is the closest visible colour to infrared, which gives a good idea of its intensity, heat and power. Red has the longest wavelength and the slowest frequency of all the colours of the spectrum.

HEALING POWER

- *Energizes*
- *Stimulates*
- *Revitalizes*
- *Warms*
- *Alleviates depression*
- *Speeds up blood circulation*
- *Speeds up the healing of infections and wounds*

It's almost impossible to ignore red. Our eyes are instinctively drawn to it. It grabs our attention, and therefore it's a difficult colour to wear if we want to melt into the background or keep a low profile. Red is associated with danger – traffic 'stop' lights are red – and also with fire, and therefore it's a colour that should be treated with respect. Too much red can be over-stimulating, leading to temper tantrums, arguments and possibly even to aggression and violence. Emotions have a tendency to become overheated and to flare up when there is an over-emphasis on red. However, you can use moderate quantities of red to fire yourself up.

It's an excellent colour to choose when you want to become more active and outgoing, more impassioned, or when you need to boost your confidence. It helps when you want to initiate new projects or make a fresh start, and its warmth and vitality make you feel good. Red is the colour associated with sex, and it enhances the libido.

positive attributes

Red promotes courage, passion, enterprise, confidence, perseverance, speed, alertness, assertiveness and vibrancy. It's the hottest of the colours, so it helps to warm you up when you're cold. When used in small quantities, it helps to ground you. For instance, it is helpful to wear red socks or shoes when you need to be grounded and in your body.

Hot and dynamic, red is not a colour to wear when we want to disappear into the background. It makes a bold statement.

negative attributes

Too much red creates restlessness, aggression and, in extreme cases, violence. Tempers can flare, leading to hot-headed outbursts or displays of temperament. Red can also lead to attention-seeking behaviour and a need to dominate social events.

when to be cautious of red

Treat red with caution around the time of the Full Moon each month, because it can make the increased lunar energy too powerful. You should also be careful of using red in colour healing if you have high blood pressure, as the condition may be exacerbated by this colour. Women should be wary of healing with red during menstruation, especially when they're bleeding heavily. Use red in moderation if you are prone to anxiety, because too much red can create a jangled, agitated atmosphere. Never use large amounts of red in colour healing, nor give it for too long at any one time.

when to use red

You'll benefit from introducing more red into your life if you're feeling listless and enervated, when it's a real effort to get yourself motivated and to take action. It's also beneficial if you're feeling tired, although you should keep it to a minimum in your bedroom because its powerful energy might interfere with your sleep patterns.

Be careful about burning red candles as they create a lot of energy. They are not suitable for contemplation or meditation.

other associations

In astrology, red belongs to the fire element and is therefore linked to the fire signs of Aries, Leo and Sagittarius. However, red has its strongest connection with Aries, and with the planet Mars. Red rules the base chakra (see pages 48–49). Its complementary colour is turquoise.

orange

Although it's a warm colour like red, orange is less hectic and fiery. It tends to glow rather than sear, and it promotes a sense of wellbeing and enthusiasm. It's more moderate than red, yet it still carries considerable power. Orange is the second colour in the colour spectrum.

Orange is a very valuable colour because it generates enthusiasm, good humour, relaxation, benevolence, generosity, expansion, playfulness, joyfulness and exuberance. Primarily, though, orange is the colour of creativity, so is an excellent choice if you want to stimulate your own innate creativity and also have the courage to express yourself in whichever way feels most suitable for you, without having to worry about what other people will think. Don't forget, though, that creativity comes in many forms, giving you plenty of scope for expressing your individuality. Orange will help you to do this, and to enjoy yourself at the same time.

This is also a very sociable colour, so orange can help you to increase your connections with other people. It's helpful if you're feeling shy or uncertain about mixing with others, because it gives you a boost of confidence. The warmth and exuberance of orange also help you to attract other people, who are drawn by the positive, extrovert energy of the colour. Relationships of all kinds benefit from the orange ray, so it's a good colour to use if you want to become more sociable or to have more fulfilling relationships. It will increase your ability to tune into others and make emotional connections with them.

Orange is a warm, vibrant colour. It helps to stimulate affection and optimism, and is a good choice when we want to cheer ourselves up.

positive attributes

Orange instils enthusiasm, togetherness, happiness, emotional warmth, optimism, forward thinking, vitality, gregariousness, creativity, the ability to achieve your potential, freedom and joy. It's warming and cheerful.

negative attributes

Too much orange creates an emotional dependence on other people and a dislike of being alone. It also triggers a tendency to be over-indulgent and to avoid responsibility. There can also be laziness and superficiality.

Orange rays are especially strong in the atmosphere at sunset. Being outdoors at this time is beneficial if we need more orange in our lives.

when to be cautious of orange

If someone already displays the positive attributes of the orange ray, there is no need to give him any more of it. In fact, it could easily be detrimental, turning his energy into sloth. Orange should also be used with care, and even then only for short periods, on people who are nervous or restless. Orange will only increase their nervous energy.

when to use orange

Orange is a wonderfully uplifting colour, so it's ideal for cheering people up when they're depressed or miserable. It's also invaluable when treating someone who is taking life too seriously, because it literally helps him to lighten up. Orange is also suitable – although only in limited amounts – when treating someone who is having difficulties in connecting with other people, and perhaps recovering from a broken love affair, as this colour enables us to make stronger emotional connections with others. You can use orange on those occasions when red would be inadvisable – perhaps for health reasons – but even so you should always use it wisely and not for too long.

other associations

Its warm colour connects orange with the fire element, and therefore with the three fire signs of Aries, Leo and Sagittarius. Orange rules the sacral chakra (see pages 50–51). Its complementary colour is blue.

HEALING POWER

- *Encouraging*
- *Revitalizing*
- *Boosts the immune system*
- *Soothes digestive problems*
- *Helps in dealing with traumatic incidents*
- *Antidepressant*

yellow

A bright and uplifting colour, yellow helps to encourage cheerfulness and a sunny, sociable temperament.

HEALING POWER

- *Stimulates the mind*
- *Aids concentration*
- *Gives mental agility*
- *Heals skin problems*
- *Detoxifies and cleanses*
- *Soothes arthritic and rheumatic conditions*

The third of the warm colours, yellow is cheerful and bright. It conjures up images of spring flowers and basking in the sunshine, and therefore helps to generate a sense of happiness and wellbeing. Above all, yellow brightens, not only emotionally and physically, but on an intellectual level as well. This is the colour that is most closely associated with the working of the brain.

Yellow stimulates our brains, leading to clarity of thought, alertness, awareness and intellectual prowess. We become more rational under the influence of yellow – especially clear, bright yellow – and our brains work more quickly. Yellow is therefore a good colour to use when you want to think clearly, whether to solve a problem or to be creatively inspired. It helps you to discriminate between your different options, and also encourages an objective and rational viewpoint. It may be too overpowering to be in a completely yellow room, but periodically focusing on a yellow object, such as a vase of flowers, helps to stimulate the brain and keep the ideas flowing. Yellow also encourages concentration, although too much yellow has the opposite effect.

Yellow is a sociable colour, because of the way it stimulates us mentally, so small doses of it are beneficial when we are attending social events. It brings us out of ourselves and helps us to find interesting things to say.

positive attributes

Yellow boosts our brains, instilling mental alertness, concentration, a detached perspective, good memory recall, clarity of thought and our overall intelligence. It's energizing, stimulating, sociable, uplifting, cheering and warming, helping us to enjoy life to the full.

negative attributes

Too much yellow creates disordered, distracted and restless thinking, making it hard to focus very clearly. A lot of yellow can also lead to social discord and arguments. It can also trigger sarcasm, exaggeration, criticism of others and a tendency to be sly or untruthful. An over-emphasis on yellow has a negative impact on the digestive system, leading to stomach upsets and an inability to absorb the nutrients from food.

when to be cautious of yellow

Yellow is very powerful and should be avoided by anyone who is suffering from nausea or a headache, because it will only make the condition worse. Be especially careful to keep away from yellowy-greens. Yellow should also be treated with caution if you're feeling jangled, agitated and restless, because it will further stimulate you rather than help you to slow down. For the same reason, you should limit your exposure to yellow if you've got insomnia or you often have nightmares.

when to use yellow

Choose yellow when you want to increase your intellectual abilities or make a decision, because it will help you to concentrate. Yellow is also very helpful if you're feeling sluggish and in need of waking up, or if you want to detoxify your body.

other associations

Yellow is the colour traditionally associated with Gemini, the astrological sign of communication. It is one of the air signs. Yellow rules the solar plexus chakra (see pages 52–53). Its complementary colour is violet.

Focusing on an yellow object, such as a yellow cup when drinking your tea, will help to stimulate the brain leading to clarity of thought.

green

Green is the colour most closely associated with nature, making us think of green leaves, plants and grass. Perhaps that's why the human eye is able to discern more shades, tints and tones of green than any other colour – we literally need green to survive.

Green lies midway in the colour spectrum between the warm and cool colours. Its position reveals its purpose, which is to create balance and harmony. Green is therefore the great restorative colour in the spectrum, helping us to calm down when we're feeling agitated and upset, enabling us to become more restful and centred. It restores our equilibrium. This is why we always feel better for being surrounded by nature. Red speeds us up but green slows us down.

This is also the colour of unconditional love, so green helps us to become more accepting of other people. It also enables us to be more compassionate towards ourselves, thereby reducing the amount of pressure that we put ourselves under. As a result, green is the ideal colour to choose when you want to improve your relationships and take people as you find them, rather than as you'd like them to be. Green helps to open our hearts, making us more affectionate and loving. We become more adaptable and easy-going when surrounded by green.

One quick way to benefit from the many qualities of green is to look out of a window at a green tree or patch of grass.

Green is also the colour of abundance and generosity. We can wear green when we want to attract more prosperity into our lives, although too much green can lead to acquisitiveness, stinginess and overt materialism. Green also encourages growth, so is a good choice if you want a situation to grow and develop.

HEALING POWER

- *Balancing*
- *Emotionally soothing*
- *Relaxing*
- *Removes stale energy from the aura*
- *Detoxifies the liver*
- *Reduces blood pressure*

positive attributes

Green fosters unconditional love, empathy, generosity and affection for others. It helps us to become more balanced and settled, and to create a stronger connection with the natural environment. Green enables us to make contact with the elemental kingdom, such as fairies and other nature spirits, as well. It attracts abundance and an ability to be grateful for what we have.

negative attributes

Too much green can lead to possessiveness and jealousy, and the desire to control other people's lives. It can also trigger envy, materialism, an emphasis on what money can buy and bitterness about the past. In addition, green can create such a strong desire for harmony that we end up sitting on the fence, afraid to express our opinions for fear of upsetting others. There can also be indecisiveness and too much passivity.

when to be cautious of green

Green stimulates growth, so you should avoid it completely when giving healing to anyone who has, or has had, cancer. You should also be wary of giving green to someone who is already indecisive, passive or afraid of upsetting others because it will exaggerate these traits. In addition, green isn't a good choice if you want to be aware of what's going on around you because it will relax you too much.

Green is one of the two colours of unconditional love. It helps us to be more accepting and appreciative of one another.

when to use green

Opt for green in healing when you want to promote relaxation, balance, unconditional love and consideration for others. Use it when you feel restricted by other people, and also when you're resistant to change.

other associations

Green is connected with all of the astrological earth signs – Taurus, Virgo and Capricorn – but particularly with Taurus. Green rules the heart chakra (see pages 54–55). Its complementary colour is magenta.

blue

If you think of the way you feel when you gaze at the blue sky during the day, you will instinctively know that blue invokes calmness, serenity and relaxation. The very act of gazing upwards into infinity helps to connect us with something greater than ourselves, and blue is a very spiritual colour. Blue is connected with the sea and the sky, both of which still contain many mysteries that we have yet to solve. There is something unfathomable and infinite about blue.

Blue is the first of the cool colours, and it has the opposite effect to red. Red creates heat and expansion, but blue creates coolness and contraction. Red objects seem closer to us than they really are, whereas blue objects appear to be further away. This means that concentrating on blue, or receiving healing with the blue ray, can help to reduce the impact of problems on us, enabling us to put them into perspective.

positive attributes

Blue helps us to become more detached from our surroundings and problems, so we see them with more clarity and perspective. It is the colour of peacefulness. It encourages tactful honesty and truthfulness, as well as stability, trustworthiness and reliability. Blue is also the colour of tradition, of steadfast and long-lasting values. It is associated with idealism, loyalty and sincerity.

negative attributes

Too much blue can lead to a sense of emotional isolation and of being disconnected from our surroundings. We become cut off from the people around us, preferring to melt into the background than to stand out in any way. We become unable to say what we think, either through shyness or because we dare not draw attention to ourselves. An over-emphasis on blue can also create a very conservative attitude, with a strong resistance to change and a mistrust of anything that seems modern or innovative.

Different shades of blue have varying qualities. Pale blue is calm and tranquil, although a very pale shade can be enervating.

We associate blue with the sky, and therefore with calmness and a sense of freedom. It is connected with the three air signs in astrology.

when to be cautious of blue

You should treat blue with great caution if you're feeling sad or depressed because it will only increase your symptoms, making you feel even more isolated, miserable, lonely and unmotivated than you were before. It is also advisable to avoid blue if you're nervous about introducing change into your life, because it will increase your need for stability.

when to use blue

Blue is excellent at combating nervous exhaustion and mental agitation. It helps to slow down our teeming thoughts, giving them more structure and clarity. Instead of feeling overwrought and jangled, we start to breathe more slowly and deeply, and to feel more calm. We can communicate properly again. Blue fosters a sense of contemplation, so is a good colour to wear or focus on when you are meditating, or when you simply want to feel more calm. It also helps to combat insomnia.

other associations

Its connection with the colour of the sky means that blue is associated with the air signs of Gemini, Libra and Aquarius. Blue rules the throat chakra (see pages 56–57). Its complementary colour is orange.

HEALING POWER

- *Calming*
- *Relaxing*
- *Encourages restful sleep*
- *Treats and cools infections*
- *Heals headaches*
- *Alleviates asthma*

indigo

If blue is the colour of the sky during the day, indigo is the colour of the sky at night. It's infinite, mysterious, velvety and deep, helping us to connect with our higher minds and our souls. Although indigo can push us out into something that's much bigger than ourselves, it can also encourage us to go within and to gain a greater sense of who we really are. With the help of indigo, we can connect with our higher purpose in life, and see the pattern of our lives from a more objective viewpoint than we might normally experience.

Indigo helps to stimulate our insight and intuition, giving us a greater connection with the atmosphere around us. The influence of the indigo ray stimulates our psychic abilities. We start to rely on our gut instincts more, and to pay greater attention to our dreams. Indigo gives us the ability to analyse our dreams, too, so we can learn from them. With indigo, we no longer only believe what we can see – we begin to trust in what we can't see, and to strengthen our links with the hidden realms.

positive attributes

In addition to helping us to increase our psychic talents and intuitive abilities, indigo enables us to increase our spiritual knowledge. We can gain a greater contact with the Divine. Indigo also enables us to strengthen our wisdom, not only learning by experience but gaining a greater sense of the particular nature of our individual spiritual quest. Like blue, indigo is a colour that gives us greater mental clarity and distance from our problems, helping us to manage them from a more mental perspective and with less emotional turmoil. It therefore helps us to make decisions, because we can stand back from them.

negative attributes

Too much indigo can lead to emotional and mental isolation, making us feel completely separated from the people and events in our lives. It can also foster a sense of spiritual arrogance, as though we know the world better than everyone else or we're privy to inside knowledge that others don't have. An abundance of indigo can lead to unfounded fears, too. There can be delusions and a tendency to idealize people, as well as to have such a high moral and spiritual code that no one can ever live up to it.

HEALING POWER

- *Increases intuition*
- *Acts as a sedative*
- *Purifies the blood*
- *Reduces physical pain*
- *Stops nosebleeds*
- *Relieves muscular tension*

Study the sky as night is falling to get a good sense of the impact of indigo. It is a mysterious colour, with great purifying qualities.

when to be cautious of indigo

Like blue, indigo should be avoided when you are feeling unhappy or depressed because it will only increase and deepen such emotions. It should also be avoided in cases of mental illness or psychic disturbance, for the same reasons. Indigo is also not a good choice for someone who is ungrounded as a result of being completely caught up in spiritual matters, especially if it seems that she has never fully incarnated into her body.

when to use indigo

Indigo is an excellent purifier and cleanser, both physically and psychically. It also has analgesic properties, and is therefore invaluable in combating pain, whether it's emotional or physical. Indigo creates contemplation and detachment from everyday concerns, so is a good colour to concentrate on during meditation, relaxation or solitude.

other associations

Indigo is associated with the astrological signs of Scorpio and Pisces, both of which belong to the water element. Indigo rules the brow chakra (see pages 58–59). Indigo has no complementary colour in the eight-colour system.

violet

Violet lies at the opposite end of the colour spectrum to red, which means it vibrates at the fastest frequency and has the shortest wavelength of all the colours. It is a highly spiritual colour, and is revered as such among many of the world's religions. At its highest, violet encourages a sense of compassion, humanitarianism and empathy for all living creatures, and also creates a bridge between humans and the inhabitants of the elemental worlds of fire, earth, air and water.

Violet helps to foster a sense of humanitarianism and to increase a consideration for all living creatures and things.

Violet takes us completely away from our everyday, human concerns, giving us a detached, enlightened and spiritual viewpoint. It therefore encourages all forms of mysticism, whether they are aligned to a particular religion or are purely personal. We are connected to our higher consciousness through violet.

Violet is profoundly connected with all forms of spirituality, and can therefore encourage us to form high ideals and ethical codes of conduct. Like indigo, it helps us to focus on our higher purpose and to gain a greater understanding of the direction of our lives. This is the colour of Divine inspiration, whether it's used artistically or spiritually. It enables us to connect with our spirit guides, and to channel their knowledge in whichever way we need.

positive attributes

Violet helps us to connect with the Divine, so we can align our human bodies with our spiritual selves. It creates a link between this world and the unseen world, so is an essential colour for psychic and spiritual work. For example, it can be used when giving all forms of healing, and it is also helpful if we want to boost our artistic and creative talents. With violet, our souls expand and our spirits soar. We can be led into acts of service for humanity.

Violet is a peaceful colour. Even gazing at some violet flowers, such as these pansies, will help to create a sense of calm and relaxation.

negative attributes

Too much violet can lead to a sense of moral and spiritual superiority, and therefore to pride. There can also be an inability to engage with purely human concerns, preferring to adopt a lofty, unemotional attitude that disconnects us from reality. Our opinions can become too abstract and hypothetical. Our compassion and humanitarian instincts give way to perfectionism and a tendency to judge others harshly for their apparent spiritual misdeeds.

when to be cautious of violet

Violet should be avoided by someone who is already very highly strung, or who is dwelling more in the spiritual realms than the human world, because it will unbalance him still further. It should also be used with caution by anyone who is depressed or who has a tendency to become very morbid.

when to use violet

Choose violet when you want to be creatively inspired or you want to make contact with your higher self. It's also a good colour if you want to find more spiritual purpose in your life, you wish to become more attuned to the needs of others or you'd like to boost your healing abilities.

other associations

Violet is linked with the astrological sign of Pisces, which belongs to the water element. Violet rules the crown chakra (see pages 60–61). Its complementary colour is yellow.

HEALING POWER

- *Aids restful sleep*
- *Clears physical and mental energy*
- *Heals ear problems*
- *Heals bacterial and viral infections*
- *Soothes scalp disorders*
- *Blood purifier*

magenta

Magenta is a colour of movement and impetus. It's a good colour to wear when we want to make changes in our lives.

HEALING POWER

- *Releases muscular tension*
- *Alleviates constipation*

Magenta is a blend of red and purple, which gives it the energy of both these colours. It therefore helps us to combine the physical energy and motivation of red with the spiritual qualities of violet. It is the colour of change, helping us to relinquish old habits and thought patterns that are no longer useful or are holding us back from the next stage in our lives.

positive attributes

Magenta helps us to attain our ideals and to fulfil our destiny. It gives us a gentle push in the right direction when we need it, and helps us to become more mature and emotionally balanced.

negative attributes

Too much can lead to a sense of superiority and an innate belief that we've got all the answers. We can become bossy, snobby and insensitive to the needs of others.

when to be cautious of magenta

Restrict your exposure to magenta if you're very restless, unsettled or changeable, because it will increase all these tendencies. You should also treat it with caution if you're finding it hard to connect emotionally with others, as it can create further distance between you.

when to use magenta

Choose magenta when you feel stuck and unable to move forward. Magenta is also very good at boosting your organizational skills.

other associations

Magenta is connected with the transpersonal point, which is one of the higher chakras of the aura. It has no astrological links. Its complementary colour is green.

turquoise

When blue and green are mixed together they create turquoise. It's therefore a combination of the harmony of blue and the serenity of green, making it a very restful and soothing colour. One of the main qualities of turquoise is its creative energy. It helps us to find a greater sense of our personal self-expression, and also gives us the confidence to express ourselves freely.

positive attributes

Turquoise fosters a sense of calmness. It enables us to cut through the endless chatter of our minds to discover what's really important and find ways of bringing it into our lives. The blue energy within turquoise also helps us to communicate better with others.

negative attributes

Too much turquoise can make us overly concerned with our freedom and individuality, so we run the risk of hurting other people's feelings.

when to be cautious of turquoise

You should treat turquoise with care if you're so wrapped up in your own little world that you give no thought to other people. Exposure to turquoise should also be limited for anyone who is over-confident.

when to use turquoise

As well as using turquoise to boost your creativity, it is also very valuable at giving emotional and psychic protection. It helps to reduce the impact that other people's energy can have on you.

other associations

Turquoise is connected with the high heart chakra. Astrologically, it has links with Sagittarius. Its complementary colour is red.

The energy of turquoise can be very beneficial when we want to communicate with others. It is a highly sociable colour.

HEALING POWER

- *Boosts the immune system*
- *Reduces inflammatory conditions*

white

Although white isn't a colour, it contains all the colours of the spectrum. When we see white, we're viewing all the energy of the visible colour spectrum. White is very bright and reflects light, and therefore white helps to illuminate dull areas in our lives. It also helps us gain new insight into situations; metaphorically it can shed light on difficulties. White encourages us to come up with new ideas.

White is associated with purity, spirituality, innocence, cleanliness and clarity. At its most positive, white is beneficial, humanitarian and wise. Its negative qualities include superiority, an inability to compromise and perfectionism.

You can use white light in healing when you aren't sure which specific colour you should use because it will contain the colour you need. White is connected with the crown chakra but has no astrological links. It has no complementary colour in the eight-colour system.

HEALING POWER

- *Useful for healing all conditions*

black

Whereas white reflects, black absorbs because it swallows up light. On a hot day, white clothes make us feel cooler but black clothes make us hotter.

Black is the colour of the soil and the deepest recesses of the night sky. It suggests infinity and mystery, and therefore it's the colour of endless possibilities. Black signifies the end of one cycle and the start of the next. For instance, seeds are planted in the dark of the soil where they sprout and turn into plants; and the time of a New Moon is known as the dark of the Moon because the lunar light isn't yet visible. Black helps us to see the possibilities inherent in new situations and to make the most of them.

The positive qualities of black include power and change. Its negative qualities include depression, despair, nihilism and a desire to abuse our power. Black is connected with the base chakra and the astrological signs of Scorpio and Capricorn. It has no complementary colour in the eight-colour system.

HEALING POWER

- *Black is never used for healing*

pink

Pink is the other colour of unconditional love (see pages 32–33). It's particularly useful for boosting energy, motivation and activity in cases where red would be inappropriate because of its strength. We create pink by mixing white and red, and it therefore contains the qualities of both colours. However, the proportions of red and white will influence the energy of a particular pink. Therefore, deep pinks carry more vibrant, motivating energy than pale pinks, which contain more white and are more soothing.

Pink is especially helpful in reducing the amount of anger and emotion contained in difficult situations, encouraging us to adopt a more gentle and understanding approach. It is an excellent relaxing colour, helping us to unwind.

Pink fosters patience, kindness, consideration and the urge to get on more easily with our fellow human beings. Its positive qualities include patience, love and the ability to care for others. Its negative qualities include over-sensitivity and a feeling of victimization. It's associated with the heart chakra (see pages 54–55) and the astrological sign of Libra. Pink's complementary colour is green of an equal colour density.

HEALING POWER

- *Muscle relaxant*
- *Helps heart conditions*

gold

Gold is a precious metal and its colour is equally cherished. It represents the highest possible spiritual wisdom and knowledge, as well as spiritual service and enlightenment. It helps us to connect with the angelic realms.

Gold is associated with the transpersonal point, which is one of the higher chakras. Astrologically, it's connected with Leo. It has no complementary colour in the eight-colour system.

HEALING POWER

- *Alleviates arthritic and rheumatic conditions*
- *Improves blood circulation*
- *Energizes the nervous system*

COLOURS AND THE CHAKRAS

Our physical bodies are composed of so much more than we might at first imagine. We tend to think that what we see is what there is, and that our bodies stop where our skin ends but, in fact, there is a lot more to us than that. Each of us is surrounded by an energetic envelope known as the aura, and permeating through that and through our physical bodies are areas of concentrated energy known as the chakras. These areas of energy consist of the major and minor chakras, as well as the higher chakras. Each of the seven major chakras is connected to a particular colour and resonates to the energy of that colour.

The previous chapter introduced you to the energies of the seven natural colours of the spectrum, as well as several other colours. This chapter will help you to apply the knowledge you've acquired to gain a better understanding of how the seven major chakras work, the colours associated with them, and how each influences us. This will give you more information about which colours to use when giving colour healing for particular ailments.

the aura and the chakras

Although our bodies appear to consist of nothing more than flesh and blood, in fact they have several energetic counterparts that together comprise our auras. Every living creature has an aura, could we but see it. Many humans can see auras as a grey or blue shimmer around a person's body or as a collection of colours and shapes.

This gift may come naturally to them, or they may be able to train themselves to see auras. Others can feel auras with their hands or can sense them intuitively. But auras exist, whether or not we can see them.

The aura is a protective electromagnetic sheath, shaped roughly like a egg, that entirely surrounds the human body, extending above the head and below the feet. It's an essential part of us and we would die without it. Within it are hundreds of tiny energy lines, called *nadis*, which transmit energy around the aura.

the auric layers

Although opinions differ, it is generally agreed that our auras consist of seven layers. The densest layer, which is the etheric body, is closest to our physical bodies and vibrates at the lowest frequency. We often see this as a thin, blue shimmer of light. Beyond this lies the emotional body, and then the mental body. The four outer auric layers – the astral layer, the etheric template, the celestial body and the ketheric template – have increasingly higher vibrations. Unless we are very powerfully clairvoyant we are unlikely to be able to see the aura beyond the mental body.

We receive the energy of colour through our auras, which is why colour healing is so effective. Our auras also hold energy, and studying a person's aura provides important information about what that individual is feeling and thinking. Repeated thoughts and feelings can get caught in the aura; if negative, these eventually turn into areas of stagnant energy that have a physical impact. This means that illnesses start in the aura and are eventually transferred to the physical body. That's why it's so important to do our best to be aware of our thoughts, emotions and motivations. We literally carry them around with us!

the chakras

Chakras are concentrations of spinning energy, points where large numbers of nadis meet within the aura. Research has shown that each chakra is located in an area of the body where there is a large concentration of nerve endings. Chakras penetrate the body energetically rather than physically, and extend outwards through the seven layers of the aura.

There are seven major chakras, which correspond to the greatest junctions of nadis, and 21 minor chakras, where fewer nadis converge. In addition, there are at least four higher chakras: the transpersonal point above the head, which links our ego with our higher self; the alter major at the back of the head, which activates our intuition; the high heart chakra, between the heart and throat chakras, which triggers our higher consciousness; and the hara, between the sacral and solar plexus chakras, which is used in healing.

Each major chakra influences the health of a particular area of the body, as well as the colour, emotions and thoughts connected with it.

The seven major chakras run down the centre of the body in a straight line. They penetrate the body and also the seven layers of the aura.

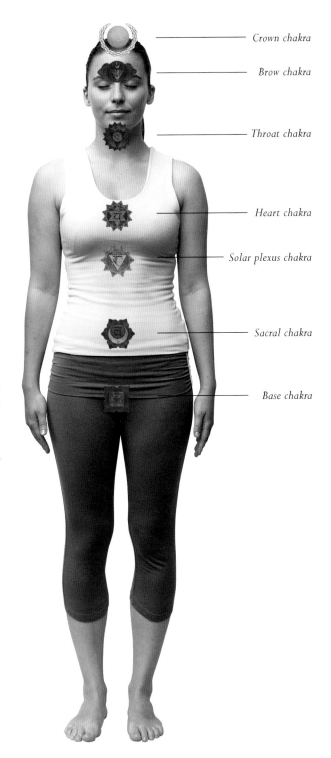

Crown chakra

Brow chakra

Throat chakra

Heart chakra

Solar plexus chakra

Sacral chakra

Base chakra

the base chakra

This chakra vibrates at the slowest rate and is connected with our most physical impulses. It is also known as the first chakra (the chakra system runs up the body and out through the top of the head). The base chakra suffuses the whole of the perineum, which is the area between the genitals and the anus.

physical functions

Because of its position in the physical body and aura, the base chakra affects the legs, the hips and the base of the spine. It is connected with structure and foundation, and therefore it's also linked with bones, muscles and skin, all of which hold our bodies together. We would be unable to survive without this bodily structure. The base chakra also affects our teeth, as well as the organs of elimination – the kidneys, rectum and bowel.

When the base chakra is sluggish or blocked, there can be problems with any areas of the body that it rules. The sacral chakra, which is the base's neighbour, will also fail to function properly because it won't receive the energy it needs.

a quick guide to the base chakra

PHYSICAL LOCATION	*Perineum*
PHYSICALLY AFFECTS	*Skeletal and muscular structures but especially the base of the spine, skin, teeth, kidneys, rectum, bowel, legs and feet*
PHYSICAL PROBLEMS	*Constipation, kidney problems, low back pain, sciatica, dental problems, varicose veins, bunions*
GLANDULAR SYSTEM	*Adrenals*
KEY FUNCTION	*Creates emotional balance*
COLOUR	*Red*

psychology

The base chakra governs our ability to materialize our goals. If we are full of fear and trepidation about what the future holds, we can't turn our dreams into reality because we lack the innate faith that will make this happen. We don't believe that the universe will support us, and we become frightened to take risks. We feel rootless and adrift. A healthy base chakra results in confidence, both in ourselves and in the abundance that the universe offers us. We feel that we belong in the world around us.

Red is the colour of the base chakra. It's a good colour to wear when we want to boost the base chakra or become more grounded.

spirituality

The base chakra is connected with the need to be grounded in reality. If we don't have our feet firmly anchored in the here-and-now, we are unable to function on a day-to-day level because we're disconnected from what's happening around us. Also, even if we yearn to connect with the highest spiritual sources, we won't be able to do that if we're ungrounded because we won't be fully aware of what we're doing.

If the base chakra is healthy, we can meet our material needs with ease and confidence. However, too strong an emphasis on the base chakra results in an overly materialistic attitude, in which ownership of people and possessions takes precedence over everything else in life.

red and the base chakra

The base chakra is aligned with the colour red. When it's healthy and spinning properly, this chakra is a clear, bright red. You may be able to see this colour physically in someone's aura or you may sense it intuitively. A muddy, dark red means the chakra is blocked with old energy and needs to be cleared (see pages 64–65). A pale, insipid red means the chakra is weak and needs to be energized.

the sacral chakra

The second or sacral chakra is located the width of two fingers below the navel. Although less dense than the base chakra, the sacral is one of the three lower chakras connected with being physically present in our bodies; the other two are the base (see pages 48–49) and solar plexus (see pages 52–53) chakras.

physical functions

The sacral chakra governs the reproductive systems of the body, both male and female. These will thrive or struggle according to the health of the sacral chakra. The sacral chakra is particularly active during puberty, when the reproductive system goes through important changes; during conception and pregnancy; and during the female menopause when radical changes are once again taking place. This chakra also affects the urinary system.

Difficulties with the functioning of the sacral chakra can also affect the solar plexus chakra, because energy won't move up the body properly.

psychology

Psychologically, the sacral chakra is connected with all forms of creativity. These can cover anything from artistic talents – when the sacral chakra works in conjunction with the throat chakra (see pages 56–57) – to physically creating a baby. However, we need to feel safe in the world before we can create anything with confidence, so a poorly functioning base chakra will have a negative impact on the sacral chakra.

spirituality

Are we open to change or are we deeply resistant to it? Are we ready to take risks or do we want to cling desperately to what we know, even if we don't like it? These are the questions posed by the sacral chakra. Very often, a rigid outlook and a resistance to change results in a rigid posture and lack of physical flexibility, especially in the hips and lower back.

Problems with the sacral chakra can also result in a reluctance or even an inability to become emotionally close to other people. This can result in loneliness and sexual frigidity, or in an over-emphasis on sex. We may also have difficulties in creating what we want in life.

orange and the sacral chakra

The sacral chakra is associated with orange. Its vibrant, warm energy is a clue to the creative nature of this chakra. Ideally, the chakra should be a bright, clear orange containing no shadows or blockages. A dark, dirty orange can indicate a difficult attitude to sex, especially if it is seen as a way of exerting power over others. A pale, watery orange signifies a poorly functioning sacral chakra, with a corresponding ambivalence to life, and a lack of creativity.

The sacral chakra, and its associated colour orange, are connected with creativity in all its many forms.

a quick guide to the sacral chakra

PHYSICAL LOCATION	*Two fingers below the navel*
PHYSICALLY AFFECTS	*Lower back, urinary and reproductive systems*
PHYSICAL PROBLEMS	*Bladder and urinary problems, infertility, menstruation and menopausal problems, prostate problems, frigidity*
GLANDULAR SYSTEM	*Gonads*
KEY FUNCTION	*Stimulates creativity*
COLOUR	*Orange*

the solar plexus chakra

The last of the three chakras connected entirely with our physical bodies, the solar plexus chakra is located beneath the ribcage in the upper abdomen. This chakra is one of the most sensitive of the major chakras because it is the storehouse of so much emotional energy. Even if you aren't aware of the other chakras in your body, you are probably conscious of this one because it's activated when your stomach lurches with fear. The solar plexus chakra can hold on to emotions provoked by a difficult event long after the event itself is over, so it is important to clear it on a regular basis.

physical functions

The solar plexus chakra helps the organs in the upper abdomen to function properly. Our stomach, liver, pancreas and gall bladder digest our food, extracting the nutrients we need, performing other vital functions and sending everything that we don't need towards the organs in our lower abdomen.

psychology

This chakra gives us drive, willpower and motivation. It helps us to make progress in our lives and to gain a sense of our own inner strength. When it's functioning well, the solar plexus chakra enables us to stand up for ourselves, to express our individuality and to be masters of our own destiny. When the chakra is blocked or sluggish, we feel powerless in the face of other people, we can't make decisions about our own lives and we let things slide.

Just as this chakra allows our bodies to physically process our food, so it helps us to process our emotions. Difficulties with this chakra can mean that our emotions get stuck – we become caught in unhealthy emotional patterns that are hard to break, especially if they began in childhood. We can't shift the anger, resentment, insecurity or arrogance that we feel, and such emotions eventually translate themselves into physical ailments that centre around our stomach region.

spirituality

Spiritually, this can be a difficult chakra, especially if we've been brought up in a religion or spiritual doctrine that practises non-confrontation and obedience. It often seems wrong to acknowledge and assert our power, to stand up to others, to refuse someone's request or to have an argument rather than to avoid confrontation. Yet these are all necessary actions at times. If we fail to react like this, perhaps through parental conditioning or anxiety about invoking bad karma, we tend to swallow the resulting anger or bitterness. This has a negative impact on the solar plexus chakra.

yellow and the solar plexus chakra

This chakra is associated with the colour yellow. Jaundice, which is one of the physical ailments connected with this chakra, turns us yellow. Cowardice, which is one of the psychological problems of this chakra, is often described as being 'yellow-bellied'. Yet a lovely, sunny yellow inspires us with hope, fortitude and the ability to be ourselves.

Ideally, the solar plexus chakra should be a clear, bright yellow. If it's murky, ochre or acid-yellow, the chakra contains energy blocks that should be removed. If it is a pale, watery yellow, the chakra isn't functioning properly and needs to be boosted. The chakras on either side of it may also be impaired.

It is a good idea to wear yellow when we want to boost the solar plexus chakra. However, too much yellow can lead to restlessness and possibly a sense of nausea.

a quick guide to the solar plexus chakra

PHYSICAL LOCATION	*Below the ribcage*
PHYSICALLY AFFECTS	*Stomach, pancreas, liver and gall bladder*
PHYSICAL PROBLEMS	*Stomach and duodenal ulcers, eating disorders, gallstones, jaundice, diabetes, cancer of the digestive organs*
GLANDULAR SYSTEM	*Pancreas*
KEY FUNCTION	*Processing emotions*
COLOUR	*Yellow*

the heart chakra

This chakra marks the midway point between the three physical chakras of the lower body (the base, sacral and solar plexus chakras) and the three Divine chakras of the upper body (the throat, brow and crown chakras). It sits in the centre of the chest, slightly to the right of the physical heart.

physical functions

As its name suggests, this chakra controls the smooth and efficient functioning of the heart. It also governs the circulation of the blood, the lungs and the body's immune system. These are all essential functions for our health; our very existence depends on them.

psychology

The heart chakra governs unconditional love. It enables us to forgive others when they hurt or disappoint us, and to take people as we find them rather than as we'd like them to be. The heart chakra also helps us to experience a universal love for everyone and everything, rather than simply for our own circle of friends and family.

a quick guide to the heart chakra

PHYSICAL LOCATION	*Centre of the chest*
PHYSICALLY AFFECTS	*Heart, circulation system, lungs, vagus nerve, immune system*
PHYSICAL PROBLEMS	*Heart disease, blocked arteries, heartburn, hiatus hernia, emphysema, lung cancer, pneumonia, bronchitis, asthma, allergies*
GLANDULAR SYSTEM	*Thymus*
KEY FUNCTION	*Stimulates unconditional love*
COLOURS	*Green and pink*

The heart chakra plays a vital role in relationships. When this chakra is working well, we are loving, affectionate, generous, joyful and warm. If the chakra isn't functioning properly, we become greedy of other people's affections, suspicious of people's motives, frightened of being rejected, intolerant and lonely. We feel the world is against us, shutting us out in the cold.

spirituality

This chakra helps us to link with the Divine through our unconditional love for all living creatures, especially when we engage the crown chakra (see pages 60–61) as well. This can seem like a tall order for most of us, yet the heart chakra helps us to show greater love and understanding towards the people in our lives and to humanity as a whole.

People whose lives are dedicated to the service of humanity, such as healers using either traditional or complementary medicine, sometimes have heart chakras that are permanently open. It's as though they are continually on call, and as a result they become emotionally exhausted and physically depleted. Sometimes it is an essential act of self-preservation to shut down the heart chakra.

When the heart chakra is weak or under-developed, the person is mean-spirited, grudging, resentful, selfish and undemonstrative.

Someone who habitually acts as an agony aunt or uncle to other people when they're in trouble should take extra care of her heart chakra.

green and the heart chakra

The predominant colour of the heart chakra is a clear, vibrant green, although it can also have pink tinges. Green is the colour of balance, echoing the central position of the heart chakra in the system of the seven major chakras. Dark, muddy green in this chakra indicates resentment and envy. If it is pale green, the person is frightened of rejection and emotional commitment.

the throat chakra

The throat chakra is the first of the three chakras that link us to the Divine and to our spirituality. It is located in the neck and is crucial to our ability to give voice to our thoughts and feelings, to communicate with others, with ourselves and with the universe. This higher chakra is one of the keys to the expression of our true selves.

physical functions

As its name implies, the throat chakra enables us to communicate with others through our voices. It therefore governs the oesophagus, the trachea, the larynx or voice box, and all the other organs of speech such as the tongue. In addition, the throat chakra affects the jaw, gums, the mouth in general and sinuses.

psychology

In addition to being able to communicate physically, the throat chakra has a major influence over what we say. Are we saying what we really think or are we simply saying what we imagine other people want to hear? Are we

a quick guide to the throat chakra

PHYSICAL LOCATION	*Throat*
PHYSICALLY AFFECTS	*Throat, thyroid, larynx, trachea, oesophagus, sinuses*
PHYSICAL PROBLEMS	*Sore throat, tonsillitis, hoarseness, problems with gums and jaw, problems swallowing, under- or overactive thyroid*
GLANDULAR SYSTEM	*Thyroid and parathyroid*
KEY FUNCTION	*Communication*
COLOUR	*Blue*

saying what's really important to us or are we blotting that out by talking about inconsequential matters instead? Do we censor our speech in some way to avoid upsetting others? Although it can sometimes be advisable not to say what we're really thinking, it will be very destructive for us if this becomes an unbreakable habit because we are then denying our true selves. This, therefore, is the main question of the throat chakra – who are we? And how can we express who we really are?

When the throat chakra isn't functioning properly, it leads to an inability to be our authentic selves. We can't express ourselves fully, leading to depression, frustration, lack of motivation and a sense of impotence.

spirituality

The spiritual message of this chakra is to communicate with honesty and to express our true selves. However, we have to do this with love and consideration to avoid blurting out things that will be hurtful and won't achieve anything. It's important to know the difference between what must be said, come what may, and what is better left unsaid.

We communicate with others through our throat chakras. When this chakra is very large and open it encourages a tendency to gossip.

When this chakra is blocked or sluggish, it's difficult for us to say what we think and feel. When it's over-developed, we define ourselves through gossip and incessant chatter. When working in tandem with the sacral chakra (see pages 50–51), the throat chakra governs our ability to be creative.

blue and the throat chakra

When it's functioning well, the throat chakra is a clear blue. Blue is considered to be the colour of fidelity, and the throat chakra asks us to be true to ourselves.

When the throat chakra is a dark blue, it indicates that its energy is blocked – probably with many impulses and ideas that have never been expressed. If the chakra is a very pale blue, the energy is weak and the person may take refuge in silence rather than dare to speak up.

the brow chakra

The brow chakra, which is located between the eyes on the bridge of the nose, is the second of the three chakras that connect us with our spirituality. Sometimes referred to as the 'third eye' chakra, it is associated with sight, our intuition and our ability to see clearly the world we live in and that which is hidden from physical sight.

physical functions

This chakra is associated with eyesight (whether good or bad), hearing, the nose and the nervous system. It is also connected with many of the brain's functions, and especially those of the lower brain.

psychology

The brow chakra encourages our intuition and inner vision – our ability to look within ourselves to discover our innate knowledge, as well as our ability to tune into the atmosphere around us and to learn from it. It enables us to tune into the spirit guides that help us through our lives. As we learn to trust our intuition and our inner sense of knowing, the brow chakra becomes more developed. Equally, because the chakras and the corresponding areas of the body are completely interdependent on one another, working to clear the brow chakra and make it stronger will help to develop the intuition.

This chakra helps us to reason and to gain a more balanced perspective of life, so we can rise above our problems and see them from a more objective viewpoint. It also enables us to understand that there is much more to life than we can experience with our five senses. Therefore, with the help of the brow chakra we see what we believe rather than believing only what we see.

spirituality

Since this is one of the three spiritual chakras, the brow chakra helps us to develop our spirituality and to become attuned to the invisible rhythms and influences that surround us. Gaining a stronger sense of the role that we are playing in our present incarnation helps each of us to understand the purpose of our life and the lessons that we can learn from it.

When this chakra is undeveloped, we are frightened to trust our intuition, having no faith in our inner knowledge. It can be difficult for us to connect with our guardian angels and the other spirits that protect us, perhaps because we don't trust our instincts when we try to make contact with them. We can also take refuge in a very rationalist approach to life, in which anything that can't be explained by science is deemed not to exist.

indigo and the brow chakra

Indigo is the colour associated with the brow chakra. The density and mystery of indigo echoes the ineffable power of our intuition. When the colour of this chakra is almost black, it signifies mental and emotional blocks which may be caused by trying too hard to develop the intuition. When it's a watery purple, there is a lack of logic.

Indigo is the colour associated with the brow chakra. Wearing small amounts of indigo helps to boost our intuitive powers, but too much can be depressing.

a quick guide to the brow chakra

PHYSICAL LOCATION	*Bridge of the nose, between the eyes*
PHYSICALLY AFFECTS	*Eyes, nervous system, ears, nose, lower brain*
PHYSICAL PROBLEMS	*Short- or long-sightedness, anxiety, poor hearing, nasal congestion, headaches, migraine, balance problems, blood clots or tumours in the brain*
GLANDULAR SYSTEM	*Pineal*
KEY FUNCTION	*Stimulates intuition*
COLOUR	*Indigo*

the crown chakra

The seventh and last of the major chakras, the crown chakra is also the last of the three spiritual chakras. Whereas the base chakra (see pages 48–49) vibrates most slowly of all the chakras, the crown chakra has the fastest vibration. It is a highly sensitive point and should be treated with care during healing. Many people feel uncomfortable when this chakra is touched or when other people get too close to it.

physical functions

Physically, the crown chakra governs the functions of the upper brain. It helps to keep our brains healthy and active. Problems with this chakra can result in mental and neurological disorders.

psychology

The crown chakra helps us in our self-belief. It helps us to formulate opinions about the meaning and purpose of our lives. When it's functioning properly, it makes us feel that we're contributing something of importance to the rest of the world and that we are here for a reason. When problems arise, we feel able to cope with them because we have faith in ourselves. We know we can ask for help – whether physical, emotional or spiritual – whenever we need it. When this chakra isn't working well, our lives lose meaning and importance. We can become despondent, apathetic and listless. Everything seems to be too much trouble, and problems are magnified because we doubt our ability to deal with them. We can even become clinically depressed because our lives are robbed of their colour and vivacity. A crown chakra that isn't functioning properly will also raise doubts about the existence of God. We may feel that God has deserted us or that we don't deserve to receive any spiritual help. On a day-to-day level, we can resent the authority that other people have over us.

spirituality

This chakra connects us to something larger than ourselves. We might call it God or we might have another name for it, but we know it's there. When the crown chakra is healthy, we feel a strong connection with the Divine, as well as with other spiritual beings. Our lives mean something. We also receive Divine help and spiritual sustenance through the crown chakra: when giving healing, we make a conscious connection with a spiritual source through this chakra. It is the gateway of the soul: at birth, the soul enters the human body through the crown chakra and it leaves through the crown chakra at the moment of death.

violet and the crown chakra

Violet is associated with the crown chakra. This is a very spiritual colour, reflecting the innate spirituality of this chakra. A healthy crown chakra is a clear, vibrant violet. When the chakra is sluggish or closed down, it takes on a very dark shade. When it's a weak violet, there is a lack of faith and an inability to trust in the Divine.

The crown chakra, whose colour is violet, is the chakra through which we connect with the Divine. It is opened in any form of spiritual work, such as meditation.

a quick guide to the crown chakra

PHYSICAL LOCATION	*On the top of the head*
PHYSICALLY AFFECTS	*Upper brain*
PHYSICAL PROBLEMS	*Brain disorders such as epilepsy, depression, mental illness, neurological disorders, anxiety*
GLANDULAR SYSTEM	*Pituitary*
KEY FUNCTION	*Connection with the Divine*
COLOUR	*Violet*

working with the chakras

Ideally, you should get used to working with your chakras for a few minutes each day. This will help you to become attuned to them, so you have a better idea of when they're functioning well and when they need attention from you.

checking your chakra colours

1 Choose a time when you are alone and won't be disturbed. Sit in a comfortable chair with both feet flat on the floor. Ground yourself by imagining that roots are growing out of the soles of your feet down into the earth. Feel them anchoring you to the earth. Mentally surround yourself in a protective bubble of golden light. Take three deep breaths, then breathe normally.

2 Tune into your base chakra. Picture its colour and shape, trusting what comes to you. You may see this chakra clearly in your mind's eye or you might simply get a sense of it. If the chakra is lopsided or out of shape, mentally adjust it until it is a spinning vortex of energy. If the colour is a murky or pale red, adjust it until it becomes a clear red. Don't spend more than one minute on this chakra or any of the others.

3 Move on to the sacral chakra and repeat the exercise, but using orange. Make any necessary adjustments.

4 Continue to work through each chakra in turn, referring to the Chakra Colour Checklist (see box opposite) to remind yourself of the colour of each chakra until they are familiar to you.

5 When you've finished the exercise, close down each chakra in turn, starting with the crown chakra – picture each chakra as a flower that's closing its petals. Then ground yourself again and once more enclose yourself in a bubble of golden light.

breathing colour into the chakras

1 Choose a time when you won't be disturbed. Sit comfortably, then ground and protect yourself (see opposite).

2 Begin with the base chakra. Picture its red colour. As you slowly breathe in, imagine the chakra being filled with clear red light. As you slowly breathe out, imagine any areas of dark or stuck energy being dispelled from the chakra.

3 Now check the colour of the base chakra again. Has it changed? Repeat the exercise, taking care to breathe light into any dark areas of the chakra. Do this no more than three times.

4 Move on to the sacral chakra and repeat the exercise. Continue with the other chakras until you've breathed colour into them all.

5 When you've finished the exercise, close down each chakra in turn, starting with the crown chakra – picture each chakra as a flower that's closing its petals. Then ground yourself again and once more enclose yourself in a bubble of golden light.

chakra colour checklist

CHAKRA	COLOUR
Crown chakra	Violet
Brow chakra	Indigo
Throat chakra	Blue
Heart chakra	Green and pink
Solar plexus chakra	Yellow
Sacral chakra	Orange
Base chakra	Red

clearing stuck energy

When you start to work energetically with the chakras, you'll soon realize that chakras can sometimes become blocked and won't function properly. A healthy chakra spins continually, while an unhealthy one spins slowly or erratically. Even if your own chakras are working well and are in balance with one another, you'll meet people whose chakras are out of alignment, with some working more strongly than others. This will be especially apparent if you start to practise colour healing and work specifically with the chakras.

One of the principal reasons for chakras becoming blocked is that they are major repositories of emotions. When we experience something unpleasant we often fail to process our resulting emotions properly. Instead of experiencing them fully, we protect ourselves (or think we do) by shoving these emotions to the back of our minds or by pretending that

chakra positive energies checklist

CHAKRA		POSITIVE ENERGIES
	Crown chakra	Connection with the Divine
	Brow chakra	Insight, intuition, inner knowledge
	Throat chakra	Communication, self-expression
	Heart chakra	Unconditional love, compassion
	Solar plexus chakra	Drive, motivation, personal power
	Sacral chakra	Joy, creativity, sexuality
	Base chakra	Confidence, security, safety

the unpleasant experience never happened. This can easily become a habit that's hard to break, and it turns into a vicious circle. The more frightened we are of facing up to life and experiencing its difficulties, the more we deny our difficult emotions and the more likely we are to run away from them in the future.

This emotional pattern soon results in blocked chakras; the stagnant emotions connected with a particular chakra will stop it spinning in the way it should. For instance, fears about love will result in a blocked heart chakra, while fears about sexual intimacy will lead to a blocked sacral chakra. Unless these energetic blockages can be cleared, they will eventually lead to physical ailments.

energizing the chakras

1 Choose a time when you won't be disturbed. Sit comfortably, then ground and protect yourself (see pages 62–63). If possible, perform this exercise while sitting in sunlight, whether outside or indoors. If that isn't possible, perform it in natural light, facing a window.

2 Spend a few minutes enjoying the warmth of the sunshine on your body. When you're ready, imagine the red energy in the colour spectrum entering your base chakra. Picture your base chakra vibrating with colour and energy. Imagine that the chakra is spinning smoothly and any blocked energy is melting away. Feel the positive energies connected with this chakra – confidence, security and a sense of abundance.

3 When you're ready, take your attention away from your base chakra and begin to focus on your sacral chakra. Feel the orange energy in the colour spectrum entering this chakra, and make a conscious effort to experience the positive energies that are associated with it – creativity, joy and emotional warmth.

4 Repeat this exercise for each chakra in turn, each time visualizing it being bathed in light from the colour spectrum and fully experiencing the emotions and responses associated with it. When you've finished, close down each chakra in turn, then ground and protect yourself as usual (see pages 62–63).

COLOUR HEALING WITH CRYSTALS

Crystals are repositories of concentrated energy. They come from deep inside the Earth, where they are created over a very long time in total darkness, so they contain the Earth's energy and are therefore very sensitive. There are many forms of crystal – some readily available and others much rarer and a lot more expensive. However, the crystals described in this chapter are easily obtainable for use in colour healing.

At first glance, you might imagine that crystals are completely inanimate objects, and that one piece of a particular crystal is exactly the same as another. However, it's been discovered that the part of the world from which a crystal comes will affect its energy. What is more, some people believe that crystals have their own form of consciousness, even though this is very different from that of the plant and animal kingdoms.

Crystals are particularly effective when their energy is linked with that of humans. If this theory makes sense to you, it will completely transform your relationship with your own crystals. No longer will they appear to be inanimate lumps of rock. Instead, you'll start to get a sense of their individual personalities. You will also take added care when selecting the crystals with which to practise colour healing, as you'll want to work with crystals whose energy blends with your own.

choosing and living with crystals

One crystal is not like another. They may look similar but they can feel very different, so you should always choose your crystals carefully. Listen to your intuition when you pick up a crystal. Does it feel good in your hand? How do you feel when you hold it? Sometimes, a crystal will seem to jump into your hand without you even knowing that you've touched it, in which case it's probably exactly the right crystal for you.

Size isn't important when choosing a crystal, so bigger isn't necessarily better. This is good news if you want to buy several crystals but only have a limited budget.

cleansing your crystals

When you've chosen your crystals and brought them home, you must cleanse them before using them. They will have picked up other people's energy during their journey from the mine where they were found to your hand, and this energy might hamper their effectiveness. You also need to cleanse your crystals whenever you've used them for colour healing.

Crystals absorb negative energies so it's important to clean them on a regular basis. Running water is ideal, provided that the crystal isn't water-soluble.

There are several methods of cleansing crystals. One is to hold each crystal under running water, although this isn't advisable for those that are water-soluble. If you don't want to risk it, you can leave the crystals in the light of the Full Moon (sunlight is equally effective but may fade them) for several nights. Another option is to bury the crystal in your garden (but do make sure that you've marked the site) or in a flowerpot of earth. Alternatively, you can mentally shower the crystal with white light, knowing as you do so that it's being cleansed of any negative energy.

dedicating your crystals

It's always a good idea to dedicate your crystal before you start working with it, so that both you and the crystal are aware of exactly what's expected of it. To do this, hold the crystal in both hands and imagine a ray of light streaming into it from your brow chakra, and then say the dedication out loud. If you wish, you can choose a general dedication that's applicable to all crystals, such as 'I dedicate you to act for the highest good for all concerned'. Alternatively, you can dedicate each crystal according to the purpose for which it's intended. For instance, if you choose a watermelon tourmaline to work with the heart chakra, you could say 'I dedicate you to radiate unconditional love at all times'. At first, repeat this dedication each time you use your crystal until you feel it's no longer necessary to do so.

One method of cleansing crystals is to leave them in sunlight for several hours. Alternatively, you can leave them in the light of the Full Moon.

living with crystals

You can use your crystals specifically for colour healing, keeping them in a special bag or box when they're not being used, or you can leave them in particular areas in your home. Rose crystal, for instance, is very effective at combating electromagnetic pollution from computers, so is a good choice of crystal to place on your desk. It's also a very nice crystal to place in your hallway so its loving energy will always greet you when you enter your home. If you want to remember your dreams, you could place an amethyst on your bedside table.

crystals for colour healing

Crystals are invaluable tools for healing, especially if you dedicate them for this purpose. Crystals come in many different colours, each of which has an affinity with a particular chakra in the body; orange crystals, for instance, respond well with the sacral chakra (see pages 50–51).

Whenever you use your crystal for healing it will absorb a lot of negative energy and you should therefore cleanse it after you've finished (see pages 68–69). However, if you keep your crystals together, and they include clear quartz and/or carnelian, these will keep all the crystals clear of negative energies.

red carnelian

crystals for the base chakra

The main colour associated with the base chakra (see pages 48–49) is red, although black is also connected with it. The following crystals are particularly effective at treating ailments connected with the base chakra.

RED CARNELIAN

This is an excellent stone for grounding and centring, and helps us to become more connected with the Earth's energies. It is also a very protective stone, guarding against negative vibrations and intentions. Carnelian heals the aftermath of abuse and provides a solid, stabilizing force, which gives us the support we need.

black tourmaline

BLACK TOURMALINE

Black tourmaline is a very powerful protector against unwanted energies, including electromagnetic pollution, negative thinking and the ill intentions of others. It helps in grounding and is especially effective when used in conjunction with red carnelian.

obsidian

OBSIDIAN

A powerful crystal that creates a strong link with the Earth's energies, obsidian is good at dissolving blockages, especially energetic blocks that prevent us from drawing the Earth's power into our bodies. It also has protective qualities so can be placed outside the home to keep away unwanted visitors.

crystals for the sacral chakra

Choose orange-coloured crystals if you want to boost or heal your sacral chakra (see pages 50–51). The following crystals are beneficial.

red beryl

RED BERYL

This is an excellent crystal for boosting creative energy and inspiration. It works at a very deep level, clearing artistic blocks and replacing them with fresh ideas. It's especially good when used in prosperity work to attract what we want in life, and it also helps to keep us optimistic and happy about the future.

TANGERINE QUARTZ

This is a very useful crystal for prosperity work because it has a cheering and constructive emotional effect, thereby making us more positive and receptive to the opportunities that come to us. On a physical level, tangerine quartz heals sexual problems, including frigidity, infertility and other reproductive disorders. It is also an excellent all-round healer.

tangerine quartz

ORANGE CALCITE

One of the most beneficial and powerful crystals, orange calcite enhances creativity and optimism. It helps us to cope with whatever life brings us, and guides us to attract helpful experiences and emotional connections. It's particularly helpful for healing problems connected with the reproductive organs. Orange calcite encourages us to release old patterns of behaviour that hold us back.

orange calcite

TOPAZ

In common with the other crystals that are suitable for the sacral chakra, topaz helps to encourage us. It attracts success in creative work, especially if this helps us to express our true selves, although of course such success won't arrive without some effort on our part. Topaz has a beneficial impact on our emotions, making us more loving and affectionate.

topaz

BROWN JASPER

This is a wonderfully grounding crystal, helping us to connect better with nature and with the world around us. It is especially useful when we feel fraught and disconnected from our surroundings, as it helps to dissolve fears and also any feelings of guilt we may be carrying. Brown jasper is recommended for healers because it balances the electromagnetic field of the aura and has good purifying qualities.

brown jasper

citrine

yellow jasper

tiger's eye

crystals for the solar plexus chakra

Yellow crystals are associated with the solar plexus chakra (see pages 52–53), and the following crystals are all good choices.

CITRINE
Although its yellow colour makes it suitable for work with the solar plexus chakra, citrine has a beneficial impact on all the chakras. It is a powerful healer and energizer, and is particularly good at combating digestive disorders. On an emotional level, it helps to clear energy blockages in the solar plexus chakra, releasing and dissolving stored-up anger. It's an excellent stone for attracting abundance.

YELLOW JASPER
This crystal has strong protective qualities, so is especially useful for protecting the solar plexus during healing and meditation. It also helps to strengthen the digestive organs, particularly after an illness. Yellow jasper soaks up pain if placed on the appropriate area of the body.

TIGER'S EYE
Tiger's eye is a very warming stone, and is especially good for healing stomach chills and other digestive ailments. It helps to boost energy and motivation, and also combats depression. Traditionally, it is said to offer protection, so helps to protect the solar plexus chakra against the draining energies of other people.

crystals for the heart chakra

Look for pink and green crystals if you want to work with your heart chakra (see pages 54–55). Although you need to feel comfortable with any crystal that you own, this is particularly important when choosing crystals for this highly sensitive chakra.

WATERMELON TOURMALINE
A very beneficial and powerful crystal, watermelon tourmaline helps to soothe and reduce all emotional difficulties, making it easier to express unconditional love and affection towards ourselves and others. It encourages a greater acceptance of situations, creating an ability to gain a deeper understanding of emotional problems and what they have to teach us. It also works on a physical level to heal the thymus.

watermelon tourmaline

ROSE QUARTZ

This is one of the most powerful crystals of all, and if you can only afford to buy a few, this should definitely be one of the crystals you choose. It's excellent for all emotional problems, whether you want to attract more love into your life or you're hoping to heal a broken heart. It's also good for physical problems related to the heart and circulation.

rose quartz

AVENTURINE

This highly protective green crystal not only guards against electromagnetic pollution, but also against people who drain us emotionally. It helps to make us more compassionate towards others while becoming less reliant on them for all our needs. It's invaluable for triggering increased creativity and inspiration.

green aventurine

crystals for the throat chakra

Choose blue crystals when you want to work with your throat chakra (see pages 56–57). This is a selection of some of the crystals that you may find useful if you want to improve the way you communicate with others.

TURQUOISE

Traditionally used to protect against negative energies and to bring good fortune, turquoise is an excellent healer of problems connected with the throat chakra, whether these are physical or psychological. It's particularly good at helping us to realize that we create our own reality, minute by minute, through our words, actions and thoughts.

turquoise

BLUE LACE AGATE

This is an ideal crystal if you're feeling blocked and unable to express yourself in the way you'd like. It will help you to become more articulate, with a better grasp of how you're thinking and feeling. It's also a very good stone for physical complaints connected with the throat and neck, such as tense shoulders and sore throats.

blue lace agate

SODALITE

Sodalite helps to clear the thoughts and calms the mind when it's racing. In addition, it helps to dissolve rigid opinions, creating a more broad-minded approach to life and helping us to appreciate other people's points of view. It's also an excellent crystal for promoting a good night's sleep, especially if placed under your pillow.

sodalite

azurite

lapis lazuli

blue aventurine

blue fluorite

blue sapphire

crystals for the brow chakra

Look for indigo crystals when you want to work with the brow chakra (see pages 58–59). These are some of the crystals that are suitable.

AZURITE
This is an excellent crystal for increasing intuition, assisting during meditation and giving protection during psychic development. It also clears the mind, helping to crystallize ideas and give greater structure to our thoughts. Azurite is also beneficial in understanding the impact that the mind has on the body, for good or ill.

LAPIS LAZULI
This very beautiful stone has a powerful impact on the brow chakra, especially emotionally and psychologically. It helps to trigger important dreams and enables us to remember and understand them. It also encourages us to speak out and to express ourselves, both creatively and in everyday situations. Lapis lazuli also protects against the influence of other people's thoughts.

BLUE AVENTURINE
This is a very useful crystal for boosting the mental processes, making sense of our thoughts and giving us the courage to say what we think. It's especially helpful for people who are frightened to venture an opinion. On a physical level, it's excellent at healing headaches, migraines, eye strain and dry eyes.

BLUE FLUORITE
Blue fluorite encourages orderly thoughts, helping us to express ourselves with clarity and precision. It increases the ability to concentrate and to focus on whatever is important. On a physical level, this crystal helps to heal problems with the eyes and ears, and is beneficial for colds, flu, sinus problems and neuralgia.

BLUE SAPPHIRE
Often contained in jewellery, such as rings and pendants, blue sapphire helps to create peacefulness and calm. It combats pessimism and depression, and encourages a much more optimistic approach to life. It can be very helpful in prosperity work, because it attracts abundance. When worn as a necklace, sapphire encourages self-expression and the ability to speak our minds.

crystals for the crown chakra

Violet and clear crystals have a strong affinity with the crown chakra (see pages 60–61). Here is a selection of the crystals you can use, some of which are also suitable for the brow chakra.

CLEAR CALCITE

This is a very useful crystal because it has so many different applications. It's excellent at cleansing and aligning all the chakras, but is especially beneficial for the crown chakra because it gives us the courage to make major changes whenever they're necessary. It helps to calm us when we're feeling emotionally wound up, and boosts concentration and memory.

clear calcite

AMETHYST

This is one of the most beneficial of all the crystals, in addition to being one of the most beautiful. It's suitable for use with the brow and crown chakras. It helps to raise the mental vibrations, connecting us with the higher realms and sharpening our intuition. It also boosts the memory and helps us to concentrate on what we're doing. Traditionally, it is used to combat the after-effects of alcohol, but is a good choice for overcoming any addiction. When placed under a pillow at night, it helps us to remember our dreams.

amethyst

MOONSTONE

As its name implies, this crystal is very receptive to the Moon's energies and it's much more powerful during the New-Full Moon phase than when the Moon is waning. It's excellent at stimulating our dreams and helping us to develop our psychic abilities. It can also be used to counteract insomnia and to reduce anxiety.

moonstone

AMETHYST HERKIMER

Amethyst herkimer helps us to gain a greater sense of the lessons that our present incarnations are giving us. It's very powerful when used as an aid to meditation or healing, and offers strong psychic protection.

amethyst herkimer

IOLITE

This is the perfect crystal when we want to initiate change in our lives, and especially when we want to rid ourselves of patterns of behaviour that no longer benefit us. When placed on the brow, it helps to relieve headaches. Iolite is also an invaluable crystal for visualization work as it stimulates the intuition.

iolite

healing with crystals

There are many ways to use crystals for healing. If you are unsure of their individual properties, be guided by their colour. You can arrange them around your home according to the atmosphere you wish to create. Hang a clear quartz crystal in the window to catch the sunlight. You can also use crystals to attract prosperity into your life, using Feng Shui principles. For instance, you could place a suitable crystal, such as citrine, in the prosperity corner of your home (the furthest rear left-hand corner from the front door).

If your choice of crystals is limited for some reason, you might like to choose a crystal that has many properties and is therefore a good all-rounder. Rose quartz, clear quartz and amethyst all come into this category.

combing out energy

One very good way to use crystals is to comb out the stagnant energy that's trapped in your aura. Ideally, you should use a single-terminated crystal, such as clear quartz, and run it through your aura close to your body but not touching it. The pointed end faces your body.

1 Ground and centre yourself (see pages 62–63). Holding the crystal by its blunt end, use the pointed end to hook out trapped energy in your aura. Do this mostly by intuition and instinct rather than by being able to see physically what you are doing. You can work through your entire aura in this way or concentrate on a particular area, perhaps because you have pain in the corresponding part of the body.

2 Continue to comb out the energy, imagining yourself unhooking, dislodging and removing it, until you feel it's time to stop. Smooth over your aura with your hands, then ground and centre yourself again.

full chakra healing

You will need one crystal for each chakra in order to perform this exercise. If you are not sure which crystals to use, read through the list of recommended crystals earlier in this chapter (see pages 70–75).

1 Choose a time when you won't be disturbed. Prepare the seven crystals by cleansing them and dedicating them for healing work. Ground and centre yourself as usual, then lie flat on the floor or a bed.

2 Place the crystal for your base chakra between your legs and imagine the energy from this crystal being transmitted to your base chakra. Focus on this for a couple of minutes.

3 When you're ready, take your attention away from your base chakra. Place the crystal for your sacral chakra on the appropriate area of your body. Feel it sending its energy into your sacral chakra to cleanse and revitalize it.

4 Continue in this manner with each chakra in turn, concentrating on each one for a couple of minutes. Leave each crystal in place throughout the healing. When you reach your crown chakra, place the crystal directly above your head on the floor or bed. Now spend a couple of minutes feeling all your chakras being energized and spinning.

5 When you're ready, pick up each crystal in turn, starting with the one for your crown chakra. Picture that chakra closing like a flower folding its petals, then pick up the crystal for the next chakra and imagine it closing up too. When you've closed your base chakra, slowly get to your feet. Ground yourself again, then surround yourself in a protective bubble of golden light.

gem essences

The usual way to work with crystals is to place them near you, under your pillow or to wear them as jewellery. However, another option is to use them to create gem essences, which greatly increases their scope.

what are gem essences?

Gem essences are an ideal way of ingesting the energy of a particular crystal. They are easy to make, but if you prefer you can buy them from specialist suppliers.

Gem essences, also known as gem elixirs, work on the same principle as flower essences and other energetic treatments such as homeopathic remedies: they contain the vibrational essence of the crystal with which they've been made. You can then drink a little of this gem essence whenever you need it.

Several companies now make gem essences, so you can buy them ready-made. Alternatively, you can make your own essences, using your own crystals. This gives you the double benefit of being able to use the physical crystal as well as drink the essence you've made from it.

how to use gem essences

If you want to take a gem essence to alleviate a temporary condition, you can add ten drops of it to a glass of water and sip it until you feel better. Alternatively, if you want to take the essence over a long period you can take ten drops four times a day. Stop the treatment when the problem has been alleviated, although you'll probably find that you forget to take the essence once your body no longer needs it.

Another option is to add ten drops of essence to your bathwater. If you do this, don't add anything else to the water, such as essential oils or flower remedies, as they may interfere with the gem essence. Or if you prefer, you can rub drops of the essence on the part of your body that you want to heal.

how to make a gem essence

This is a very simple procedure. All you need is the crystal that you want to work with, a clean glass bowl, a clean glass bottle, an unopened bottle of still mineral water and some brandy or organic cider vinegar. Make sure that the crystal isn't water-soluble and doesn't contain a poison such as lead, sulphur or copper.

1 Before you start, make sure that your chosen crystal has been cleansed because you will be transferring its energies to the mineral water. Wash it under lukewarm running water until you sense that it's completely clean. If you wish, you can programme it to create an effective essence.

2 Place the crystal in the glass bowl and cover it with the mineral water. Use just enough water to submerge the crystal. Cover the bowl with clingfilm and leave on a sunny windowsill for 12 hours.

3 Remove the crystal and pour the energized water into a clean glass bottle. If you want to keep the gem essence for several days or weeks, you must preserve it by adding one measure of brandy or organic cider vinegar to every two measures of the energized water.

4 This essence is the mother tincture, which you can dilute further if you wish. Put ten drops of the tincture into 30-ml (1 fl oz) brown dropper bottles and top up with brandy or cider vinegar. Make sure you label the bottles clearly!

gem essence remedies

CRYSTAL	REMEDY
Amethyst	Cure addictions; dreamwork
Rose quartz	Foster unconditional love; heal relationships
Clear quartz	All-round healing
Blue lace agate	Making fresh starts

COLOUR HEALING WITH THE ELEMENTS

In this chapter you will learn how to take your colour healing treatments one step further, using some of the techniques used by professional colour healers. The techniques in this chapter involve using the elements of fire, air and water for healing purposes, and they vary in complexity from the very simple to being rather more complicated. Nevertheless, most of the techniques are easy to apply at home, using very simple equipment. You can even make some of this equipment yourself.

You might wish to visit a professional colour healer to experience fully some of the treatments in this chapter, such as colour healing with light. This is a complicated treatment and is much stronger than any other therapy described in this book. As a result, it should be treated with great respect and with a certain amount of caution.

Whichever treatments you wish to give yourself, always remember the rule that you must use the complementary colour or hue in addition to the main one that you've chosen. This will create the necessary balance within your body, and prevent you absorbing too much of one colour and too little of its opposite.

solarized water and oils

Solarization is a very gentle yet highly effective process in which you leave water or oil in sunlight to impregnate it with the Sun's rays. Although solarization relies on sunshine, you can perform this technique on overcast days too, because the rays are present even if we can't see them. However, you can't solarize oil or water at night because the Sun has set and is therefore shining in the opposite hemisphere to the one in which you live.

Always solarize the water or oil with the particular colour that you think you need. For instance, if you believe that you need the colour orange, perhaps because you're feeling listless and dispirited, you can treat yourself with water or oil that has been infused with particles of orange light. You can drink small quantities of the water, or rub the water or oil on an affected area of your body. Another option is to put a few drops of the solarized liquid in your bathwater.

making solarized water or oil

This is a very simple process, although it calls for a certain amount of forward planning, but only by a few hours. Ideally, you should prepare a relatively large quantity of the water or oil and then store it in a screw-top bottle in the refrigerator. The water will stay fresh for two or three days, whereas the oil will stay fresh for longer. Even so, it's best to use it as fresh as possible, so it retains plenty of the Sun's energy.

You can make a solarized liquid in one of two ways: either place it in a glass container of the required colour, or you can place it in a clear glass container that you then surround with a cellophane filter in the colour you want to use. Always use a glass container, as water in a plastic container will be tainted by the plastic's energy. When the time is up, you can either use the water or oil immediately, or you can store it for future use. Either way, you only need to use a few drops at any one time because it is very potent.

1 Ensure that the glass container is completely clean. Fill it with still spring water or your chosen oil. If you're using a coloured glass container, cover the top with a sheet of plastic wrap and place it in direct sunlight. Leave it for three hours on a sunny day or in the summer. Leave it for eight hours in the winter.

2 If using a plain glass container, wrap it in the coloured cellophane filter of your choice, securing it with tape. Cover the top of the container with another piece of the cellophane filter. Place in direct sunlight. Leave it for three hours on a sunny day or in the summer. Leave it for eight hours in the winter.

3 Preserve the water by mixing a small amount of it 50/50 with brandy or organic cider vinegar and then decant into a brown dropper bottle. Keep the water in the fridge. The oil doesn't need to be preserved but you should keep it out of sunlight to prevent it oxidizing. Always remember to label the bottles so you know which colour they contain.

suitable oils

You can use any oil you wish for this process, although you should try to ensure that it's as pure as possible. You might like to choose an organic oil. The oil is only for external use, but even so it pays to choose carefully. Carrier oils such as sweet almond oil are ideal, although you can use cold-pressed olive or sunflower oil if you wish.

drinking solarized water

You only need a few drops of solarized water to feel its effects. Ideally, you should take four drops, four times a day, each time putting the drops straight into your mouth. However, make sure that you don't touch your mouth with the dropper because that will transfer germs to the water.

When you drink the solarized water, it will help if you visualize yourself absorbing the relevant colour at the same time. For example, if you've solarized the water with the orange ray, you should imagine the colour orange spreading through you as you drink the water. Feel its warmth and vitality affecting every cell in your body.

Don't forget that the warm colours of the spectrum – red, orange and yellow – all have an energizing effect on the body. You should therefore try to avoid treating yourself with these colours shortly before going to sleep as they will make you feel wide awake. Equally, blue, indigo and violet are the cooling and calming colours of the spectrum, and will therefore help you to slow down and relax. You might wish to avoid these colours when you need to be alert and active.

other uses for solarized water and oil

In addition to drinking solarized water, you can apply it to your body. Rub a few drops of the water or oil on the area of your body that corresponds to the colour you've chosen. For instance, you can rub green or pink water or oil on the area around your heart chakra if you want to heal emotional problems or encourage unconditional love within yourself.

You can also apply the liquid directly to an area of your body that needs physical healing, choosing the colour that corresponds to the ailment you want to treat. For instance, if you have an irritated scalp you can rub in a few drops of violet solarized water several times a day. You could also use violet water or oil as an analgesic, to reduce pain in your body. If you've burned an area of your body, you could treat it with a cold compress that has been soaked in blue solarized water.

Another use for solarized oil or water is to have a bath in it. You only need to add a few drops to the bathwater, but you should ensure that you don't add anything else to the water, such as an essential oil, in case its energies conflict with that of the solarized water. Although it can be beneficial to use the solarized water or oil in this way, you should not use the same colour continuously because that will unbalance your body's energy.

If you're going to use the solarized oil or water on a regular basis, you should make some in the complementary colour as well, so you can give yourself a completely balanced treatment. However, this is not so important if you're only going to be using the solarized water or oil once or twice.

colour visualization cards

One very helpful way to work with colour is to visualize the colour that you need and mentally soak yourself in its energy. Some people find this easy and some find it almost impossible simply because their minds don't work that way.

If you belong to this latter category, you can help yourself tune into the different colours you need by making colour visualization cards. These don't have to be very big. They simply need to be accurate representations of the colours you need. When you've made them, you'll find that you can use them in many different ways for colour healing.

making colour cards

First, you need some stiff white card. If you're working with the seven-colour system of colour healing (red, orange, yellow, green, blue, indigo and violet), you need to make seven colour cards. If you're using the eight-colour system (red, orange, yellow, green, blue, turquoise, violet and magenta), you should make eight cards. Make sure all the cards are exactly the same shape and size, as you will want to shuffle them when you use them. Draw either a circle or a square on each card, leaving a border of white outside the image. Paint the square or circle with a single colour. You can use acrylic, oil or watercolour paints, or you could use crayons, oil-based pastels or anything else that appeals to you. Whichever art medium you choose, you should select colours that are as bright and clear as possible. Avoid any colours that are dark and muddy or too pale, because they won't be the true colours that you want.

how to use the cards

Let your imagination and intuition guide you into making the best use of these cards, but here are some suggestions.

Daily reading Shuffle the cards, with their blank side uppermost so that you cannot look at them. Alternatively, you can place them face-down on a flat surface and shuffle them around. When you're ready, mentally ask for guidance about how to make the best use of the day ahead, and then choose one of the cards intuitively without looking at them. The colour you choose will tell you which energies you need for the day to come. For instance, if you choose green it means that you need to remain balanced and calm. It might be a good day to surround yourself with nature, or to give someone healing. Alternatively, you might wish to do something else that is connected with the colour green. On the other hand, if you selected the colour red, that would tell you that it's a day for being energetic, for starting new projects and for showing courage when necessary.

Answering a question You can also use your colour cards to answer a question that's been puzzling you. For instance, if you're coping with a difficult situation you could ask for information about how best to handle it, and then approach it according to the nature of the colour you pick. Violet, for example, would tell you to trust your intuition, to express compassion towards others and to call on your spirit guides to help you.

colour meditations

Energy follows thought. Therefore, you only have to think of something to benefit from its energy. If you don't have access to a particular colour when you feel in need of it, you can imagine it instead. For instance, if you're feeling tired but you've got to do something energetic, you can imagine that your body is being bathed in red light. Equally, if you are very wound up and anxious, you can imagine yourself being suffused with blue light to calm you down.

flower meditation

This is an excellent way to heal yourself with a particular colour. You can use it in conjunction with any of the other colour healing treatments in this book or you can use it by itself.

1 Choose a time when you won't be disturbed. Sit in a comfortable chair with your spine erect and your feet flat on the floor. If your feet don't reach the floor, place a pillow or cushion beneath them. If there are other reasons why your feet can't reach the floor, simply imagine that they can do so.

2 Take several deep breaths, releasing all tension with each out-breath, so you feel relaxed, then breathe normally. Ground yourself in the usual way (see pages 62–63), and mentally surround yourself with a protective bubble of golden light.

3 Imagine that you are in a favourite place in nature. Take time to hear the birds sing, feel a light breeze on your face and smell the fresh, pure air. Look around you until you see a path. Walk down this path until you reach a gate that leads into a garden. Open the gate and close it behind you.

4 Walk around the garden. It is very beautiful, with beds of lovely flowers. There is also a seating area. Walk among the flowers until you see one with the colour that you need. If you don't know which colour to choose, ask to be shown the flower you need. Pick this flower, knowing that you aren't harming the plant, and carry it over to the seating area.

5 Inhale the delicious scent of the flower you've picked. As you breathe in, imagine the colour of the flower flooding your aura and every cell in your physical body. Really feel this happening, and notice the resulting change in your energy. Continue to inhale the scent of the flower for a couple of minutes.

6 When you're ready, return to the flower borders and pick a flower in the complementary colour to the first one you chose. Return to the seating area and repeat the exercise with the second flower.

7 After a couple of minutes, thank the flowers for their help, then leave the garden and close the gate behind you. Walk back down the path until you reach the place where you began the meditation.

8 Now begin to count backwards from five. With each number, you are gradually becoming more alert and aware of your surroundings. By the time you've counted down to one, you are completely awake and back in your chair. Ground yourself again, and close down your chakras (see pages 62–63).

contact healing with colour

One of the most powerful yet gentle ways to use colour is to apply it through contact or hands-on healing. In this process, you direct colour into another person's body so it suffuses every physical cell and also soaks into her aura. You can control the amount of colour you send, and the colour itself, and you don't need any special equipment. All you need is a pair of hands (although even these can be optional) and a loving heart.

When practising colour healing, the healer visualizes a suitable colour as the healing energy flows out through her to the patient.

how to be a healer

If you've never consciously given anyone healing before you may wonder how you go about it. However, it's highly likely that you've already practised healing thousands of times, without being aware of it. Giving someone a hug when they're upset, rubbing your elbow when you bang it or telling a child who's cut his finger that you'll kiss it better are all ways of giving healing.

Healers have different ideas of how the healing energy works, but many agree that it flows through them rather than being generated by them. For many healers, the healing energy comes from the highest source of Divine power that they can imagine. It flows down through the crown chakra, through the body and out through the heart chakra and the minor chakras in the palms of the hands. If you practise colour healing in this way you will benefit from the healing energy as it passes through you and you won't exhaust yourself by using your own energy. In fact, you'll probably feel invigorated after the healing session is over. Many healers believe that it is tiring to generate the healing energy within yourself, rather than channelling it from a higher source.

what is contact healing?

In contact healing, you use your hands to send healing energy to another person's body. Although the process is called contact healing, it usually involves holding your hands several centimetres or inches away from the person's body. The energy from your hands will be transmitted easily through the other person's energetic body (her aura) into her physical body. She may experience this as a tingling sensation, as heat or as coolness. Alternatively, she may not feel anything at all but that doesn't mean you aren't sending her healing – it simply means she isn't aware of it for some reason. Energy follows thought, therefore focusing on sending someone a particular colour means that she will receive that colour.

choosing the right colour

During the contact healing you will be consciously flooding your patient's body with colour. Which colour should you send? If you know that she has a particular ailment you can select the appropriate healing colour, as described in *The power of colour*. Before you do this, though, you must always check that the colour you've chosen is suitable. For instance, if someone is recovering from an operation you might want to send her the colour red to encourage her scar to heal quickly. However, you might also know that she has high blood pressure, in which case red isn't a suitable colour for her. Green, however, will help to reduce her blood pressure and also soothe her wound. You should then send her magenta as the complementary colour.

Alternatively, you can wait to see which colour comes into your mind when you begin the healing session. Trust your intuition when this happens, but be guided by common sense. For instance, you should always be careful about sending someone red because it's such a strong and powerful colour. Always finish the session by sending out the complementary colour. However, if this is red and you want to avoid it, you can send pink instead. Whichever colours you send, you must ensure that they're clear, clean and bright. Don't send muddy or pale colours.

If you still aren't sure which colour to use, or you're worried about choosing the wrong colour, you can send someone white light instead. This contains every colour of the spectrum, and the other person's aura and body will absorb the colours that are needed.

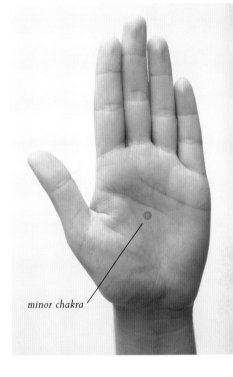

minor chakra

During contact healing, healing energy travels out through the minor chakra located on each hand in the centre of the palm.

giving contact healing

Choose a time when you won't be disturbed, and when neither you nor your patient is in a hurry. Make sure the room is warm and comfortable, with no distractions. Your patient can either lie on a couch or bed, or sit in a chair.

1 Start by grounding and protecting yourself (see pages 62–63). Now imagine that your crown chakra has opened and it's receiving a ray of healing energy from the highest source you can think of. Feel this healing energy enter and begin to seep through your body. You are now ready to start the healing.

2 Concentrate on the area of your patient's body that needs healing. Hold your hands a couple of centimetres or inches away from this area. Imagine that the healing energy, in the colour that's most appropriate, is pouring down from the highest source into your crown chakra and out through your heart chakra and the palms of your hands. Know that this colour is flooding your patient's aura and physical body, and giving her the healing she needs.

3 You may have to move your hands further away from her body if she feels extreme heat or cold. Alternatively, your own instinct may guide you to move your hands away at a certain point. Let your intuition tell you when the healing is complete. You should now send out the complementary colour in exactly the same way as before, to balance the healing and ensure that your patient has received the energies she needs.

4 When you've finished sending the complementary colour, the healing is complete. Ask your patient how she's feeling, in case she's experiencing any discomfort that you can alleviate. Ground her by placing your hands on her feet and imagine that roots are growing out of the soles of her feet into the earth. Now mentally close down each of her chakras in turn, starting with the crown chakra, and then enclose her in a bubble of golden light. Step away from her and imagine that you're being bathed in a shower of light. Then ground yourself, close down your own chakras, also starting with the crown chakra, and surround yourself in a protective bubble of golden light.

absent healing

You can give someone colour healing even if she isn't with you in person. Simply say her name, either mentally or out loud, and then imagine sending her the colour that you think she needs. Allow your mind to be filled with this colour. Then send out the complementary colour. When you've finished, ground yourself and close down your chakras in the same way as for contact healing.

coloured light

A full-spectrum light box helps to alleviate the depressive condition known as Seasonal Affective Disorder, or SAD.

Colour healing has been a part of allopathic medicine in the West since the end of the 19th century. The Danish doctor Niels Finsen (1860–1904) discovered that ultraviolet light impeded the action of bacteria. He used red light to inhibit the formation of smallpox scars, and later treated tuberculosis and lupus with coloured light.

Since the 1960s, babies born with jaundice have been treated in hospital with visible light phototherapy. The tiny child (with his eyes covered for protection) is continually bathed in coloured light for several days until the jaundice abates. The light is absorbed through the child's skin and enters the bloodstream, where it breaks down the bilirubin, an excess of which causes jaundice, into products that can easily pass through the system. It's been found that blue light is the most effective treatment.

The latest form of phototherapy involves covering the child with a special blanket that contains lights woven into the fibres of the fabric. The actual method may have changed but the thinking behind it remains the same – coloured light has powerful healing properties.

Skin problems, such as eczema and psoriasis, are sometimes treated with ultraviolet light. Colour is also used to treat some cancers, using a system called Photodynamic Therapy (PDT), which was developed by Dr Thomas Dougherty in the US. A light-sensitive compound is injected into the patient's body, where it accumulates in the cancer cells. When the compound is exposed to red light (chosen because it has the longest wavelength and is therefore able to penetrate tissue more deeply than any other colour), it and the cancer cells are destroyed.

living with SAD

Most people feel lighter, more cheerful and more energetic when the Sun shines, and less so in the winter. For some, though, this effect is exaggerated and winter is a time of depression, when they truly want to hibernate. They lack energy and motivation, feel excessively sleepy and crave carbohydrates. This condition is known as Seasonal Affective Disorder, or SAD, and can have a severe impact on the quality of a person's life. It is easily treated, however, with full-spectrum light. This often contains ultraviolet light, so it mimics the energizing action of sunlight. Someone with SAD sits near a special light box for up to four hours each day during the autumn, winter and early spring when the amount of available sunlight is poor.

Even if you don't have SAD yourself, you might still benefit from a full-spectrum light box, especially if you spend a lot of time indoors in artificial lighting. For instance, you might work at nights so spend a lot of your day sleeping or work in a large office where the lights are on all day long. Such environments are known to deplete physical energy, to increase irritability and fatigue, and to cause depression.

Skin disorders, such as eczema and psoriasis, are often treated with colour light therapy. However, this should only be practised by a qualified professional.

If you think you would benefit from treatment with a light box, you should consult your optician first to check that you don't have any eye conditions, such as glaucoma or a disease of the retina, that might mean it's unsuitable for you.

professional colour healing

You can consult a professional for colour light therapy. This involves the use of special full-spectrum lights that are fitted with coloured filters. Colour light therapy should only be administered by someone who has been fully trained – it's not something that you should attempt at home.

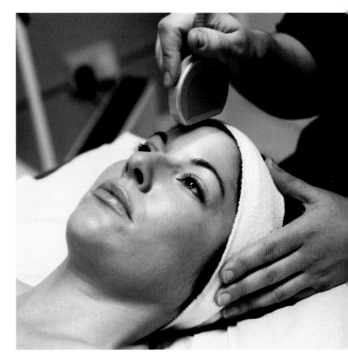

colour healing with fire

You can successfully give yourself colour healing with the aid of fire. Fire should always be treated with respect, so be careful when using lighted candles and never leave naked flames unattended. You should also take care to keep candles away from fabrics, such as curtains and bed linen.

coloured candles

If you want to cleanse a room with the help of a candle, you should choose the colour carefully. A violet candle is ideal since it is excellent at both purifying and clearing atmospheres.

One excellent way to introduce colour into your living space is to burn a candle in the appropriate colour. This is especially effective if you want to cleanse the atmosphere in a room after an argument or any other disruptive and difficult experience. If you've just moved into a new home, you can cleanse the atmosphere and then consecrate the space with a lighted candle. Picture any negative or discordant energy being burnt away by the candle flame.

It makes sense to choose the colour of candle that's most suitable for the task you've set it. For instance, if you want to purify the atmosphere of your room, perhaps before practising meditation or healing, you could light a violet candle. If you want to evoke more compassion within yourself, you could light a pink candle. To calm yourself after a hectic day, light a blue candle. If you want to increase your knowledge and understanding, burn a yellow candle.

It's perfectly acceptable to burn a candle that you've already used for the same purpose, but it's not advisable to expect one candle to perform a different function each time you light it. For instance, if you burned a pink candle while you were entertaining some friends, you shouldn't reuse it to create a more loving atmosphere when you're sitting alone.

It's a good idea to cleanse the candle before you burn it, either by imagining that you're showering it in white light or by burying it in a container full of sea salt overnight. When you're ready to extinguish the candle, either pinch out the flame with your fingers or use a candle-snuffer.

burning essential oils

Another way to introduce more colour into your life is to burn aromatherapy oils in a special burner. You can buy these burners from many health food shops, as well as over the internet. They have space for a small nightlight that sits beneath a bowl in which you place four or five drops of your chosen essential oil mixed with water. The gentle warmth from the candle flame helps to diffuse the volatile particles of essential oil into the atmosphere, thereby sending out the colour associated with the particular oil. You also have the benefit of enjoying the delicious scent of the essential oil!

oils and their colours

Each essential oil is connected to a specific colour, either because of the action of the oil (such as warming, cooling or antiseptic) or because of the colour of the flower or plant from which it is distilled. Essential oils are best avoided during pregnancy because many can trigger uterine contractions; only use them under the guidance of a qualified aromatherapist.

An aromatherapy burner will fill a room with the fragrance of an essential oil. It pays to choose a good-quality oil, as this will have the best scent.

essential oils by colour

COLOUR	PLANT
RED	Rose geranium, cinnamon, black pepper, cajuput
ORANGE	Neroli, mandarin, allspice, camomile, cedarwood, juniper
YELLOW	Rosemary, grapefruit, lemon, basil, clary sage, fennel
GREEN	Pine, eucalyptus, melissa
BLUE	Marjoram, peppermint, cypress
INDIGO	Lavender, palmarosa, vetiver
VIOLET	Tea tree, frankincense, myrrh, ylang-ylang

coloured fabrics

One of the classic ways to give and receive colour healing is to use coloured fabrics – long pieces of loosely woven silk, cotton or wool that are draped over the body until the aura has absorbed the energy of the particular colour.

When working with colour in this way, it's important to use natural fibres. Man-made fibres, such as polycotton and nylon, are available in every colour but they don't allow the skin to breathe and they don't transmit the energy of colour in the same way as natural fabrics.

finding the fabric

Use this colour wheel to check the complementary colour of the fabrics you are using for this form of colour healing.

You can buy special coloured silks for this form of colour healing, or you can buy suitable pieces of fabric whenever you see them. Make sure that the piece of fabric is long enough to stretch from your neck to your toes.

Keep track of the colours you've collected and make sure that you have as wide a range as possible. It is important to balance the colour you've chosen with its complementary colour. Ideally, you should buy a particular colour and its complementary colour at the same time, to ensure that you have them both.

choosing the colour

When you're ready to give yourself a colour treatment, choose the colour of the fabric according to your need at the time. Make sure that you've got its complementary colour as well.

cleansing the fabric

The coloured fabrics will absorb a lot of energy from your aura so you should cleanse them after use. If it's impractical to wash them, you can take them outside and shake them several times. Hang them on your washing line on a breezy day so the air can get to them.

giving yourself a colour treatment

Choose a time when you can fully relax and absorb the colours of the fabrics. It's preferable to perform this exercise in natural light, rather than artificial light – performing it in sunlight, whether inside or outdoors, is ideal.

You can do this exercise naked if you wish. If you prefer to wear underwear, make sure it's white cotton to avoid compromising your treatment with a third colour. Alternatively, you can wear a white cotton dressing gown. You will have to time yourself, so have a stopwatch or some other timer ready.

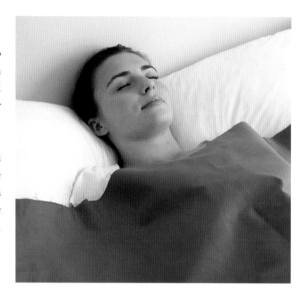

1 Lie down on a flat, comfortable surface such as your bed, but cover it first with a white sheet. Cover yourself with the fabric in the colour of your choice. Set the timer for 20 minutes. While you are lying under the fabric, concentrate on absorbing the energy of the colour you've chosen.

2 After 20 minutes, remove the fabric and replace it with one in the complementary colour. Set the timer for another 20 minutes. Once again, concentrate on absorbing the energy of this colour.

3 When the time is up, allow a few seconds for you to come back fully into your body. Close down your chakras and ground yourself in the usual way (see pages 62–63), then stretch your arms and legs, and get up slowly.

Try to avoid man-made fabrics because they don't transmit the energy of colour in the same way as natural fabrics.

COLOUR HEALING IN YOUR HOME AND GARDEN

It is especially satisfying to practise colour healing every day in as many forms as possible. By now, if you've followed the exercises in this book, you will have started to transform your relationship with colour, with the result that colour healing is becoming second nature to you. Instead of taking the different colours for granted or not paying much attention to them, you are now becoming much more aware of the impact that they have on you. You will find that the more you work with colour, the more sensitive to it you'll be.

It's time to turn your attention to the colours in your home – the colours you live with every day. Consider the effect they have on you. Do you respond best to the stimulating colours of red, orange, pink and yellow? Are you happiest with neutrals, such as green or white? Or are you drawn to the cooler colours of blue, turquoise, indigo and violet? This chapter will help you to choose suitable colours for the rooms in your home, and also give you ideas about how to continue this theme into your garden or balcony. You will also discover how to use colour healing in your diet, so you always eat the foods that your body needs. Above all, you will learn how to use your intuition to bring the appropriate colours into your life.

create a colour healing garden

You don't have to be an ace gardener to create a colour healing garden. You don't even have to own a garden: you could fill your home with flowering pot plants, turn your balcony into a mini botanical garden or invest in some window boxes. All you need is a little ingenuity and a feel for the colours you'll be working with.

sharing your garden with others

If you share your home with other people, you will have to share your garden as well. If the rest of the household isn't keen on the idea of you turning the entire garden into a healing paradise, you may have to negotiate taking over a small corner of the garden so you can do whatever you want with it. If this happens, don't be surprised if the people you live with start to visit your healing garden on a regular basis. Your efforts may turn out to be so successful that in time you'll be invited to work your magic on the rest of the garden.

single-colour gardens

Plants are just as beneficial inside our homes as they are in our gardens. Flowering pot plants add instant colour and vibrancy.

The most effective colour healing gardens are designed around a limited palette of colours. A garden that's a hectic jumble of colour will be great if you need to perk yourself up and become more energized, but it won't be what you need if you're looking for rest and relaxation – it's more likely to have a jarring effect on you.

You need to think about the colours you require from a healing perspective and concentrate solely on them. For instance, if you've been lacking motivation recently you might be inspired to create a garden in reds and oranges. These fiery colours will have an energizing impact on you, so much so that you may spend more time working in your garden than relaxing in it. The green foliage will help to counteract what might otherwise be far too strong a concentration of red and orange. (perhaps leading to irritability or over-excitement).

This soothing border concentrates on the violet end of the spectrum, with the occasional white flower to provide contrast.

If you long for a garden in which you can be restful and contemplative, you could concentrate on white. A blue garden would be an excellent choice if you're feeling rushed by life and you value every second you get for some peace and quiet. If you live with a lot of chronic physical pain, a violet and purple garden will help to soothe you and may even reduce the amount of pain you're experiencing.

If you don't need any particular form of healing but you would love to create a colour healing garden, simply let your intuition choose the colour that is most appropriate for you. This might be dictated by the colours already in your garden, a favourite species of flower, a favourite season or the colour you love best.

The scarlet of these pelargoniums is balanced by their green leaves. They are best used in small amounts to avoid them becoming overpowering.

complementary colours

Don't forget the rule about using complementary colours in colour healing. You can do the same with a healing garden, by planting yellow and violet flowers, for instance. However, if you've got your heart set on a single-colour garden you can rely on the green of the foliage to act as a complementary colour. Green is a perfect balancing colour, and will balance any other colour that you use. Of course, green is the complementary colour of magenta, so if you've chosen to create a pink and magenta garden, the green foliage will be the natural complement to it.

low-maintenance gardens

Unless you're a dedicated gardener who likes nothing better than to put on your gardening gloves and sally forth with your trowel, or you can pay someone to maintain your garden for you, try to make your healing garden as low-maintenance as possible. Sitting in your little oasis of tranquillity won't be a restful experience if you're continually aware of the perennial weeds smothering your carefully chosen plants.

inspiration

There are plenty of gardening books and magazines to give you ideas about what to plant in your healing garden. Ideally, though, you should visit a selection of gardens so you can get a true picture of how you react to the different colours. This will help you to discover which colours you are drawn to and whether any colours repel you. How do you feel when you walk through a bluebell wood in spring? Would you like to reproduce that feeling in your own garden?

If you get the chance, research some famous gardens. Not only will these help you to experience the effect that the colours have on you, but they will also give you ideas about what to plant in your own garden. For instance, in the world-famous Sissinghurst garden in Kent, England, Vita Sackville-West and her husband, Harold Nicolson, created an all-white garden and a sunset garden of reds and oranges. Pay them a visit, or look at their photographs in some gardening books, to see if they appeal to you.

adding other touches

If you have the space, you can add other touches to your garden. A garden designed to create a sense of peace and tranquillity, for instance, cries out for a comfortable seat on which you can relax. If you decide to buy yourself a deckchair, make sure it's in a suitable colour. For example, it might be the same colour as the main theme of your garden or it could be the complementary colour.

Involve as many of your senses as possible so that you become completely engrossed in your garden and it brings you the maximum benefit. Choose scented flowers where possible, or aromatic foliage that you can rub between your fingers. Find plants that are particularly attractive to bees, butterflies or other insects, to bring life and energy to your garden. Many herbs fulfil both these functions, being aromatic and good hosts to insects. You will also have the benefit of being able to pick and eat them.

Ideally, a healing garden should be somewhere peaceful, relaxing and tranquil, where the cares of the world don't intrude. Mobile phones are definitely out of bounds!

You could install a modest fountain or a small pond if you like the sound of running water or you want to attract plenty of wildlife into your garden. Running water is especially restful in an all-green, blue or mauve garden because it will increase the sense of tranquillity. If you'd like a productive garden, you could plant suitably coloured vegetables among your flowers. However, do try not to turn your healing garden, which is intended to be enjoyed, into a chore that needs your continual attention.

You may want to make this part of your garden organic, even if you use chemicals in the rest of the garden. By tuning into your healing instincts you will feel more sensitive in your colour healing garden, and probably want it to be as natural as possible.

plant suggestions

Your choice of plants will depend on several factors, including the type of soil, whether it's moist or dry, the direction the garden faces and its microclimate. Another very important point to consider is your level of expertise. If you aren't an excellent gardener, don't let yourself be seduced into buying beautiful plants that are tricky to maintain and which die the moment your back is turned. It will be far better to go for simple but beautiful everyday plants that are able to look after themselves, such as herbaceous perennials.

Browse through an encyclopedia of plants or visit a local plant nursery to get lots of ideas. In the meantime, here are some suggestions for plants that you might like to consider.

plant suggestions by colour

RED AND ORANGE

Tropaeolum majus 'Tom Thumb'
Love-lies-bleeding (*Amaranthus caudatus*)
Wallflower (*Erysimum*)
Tulip (*Tulipa*)
Oriental poppy (*Papaver orientale* 'Allegro')
Firethorn (*Pyracantha*)
Japanese quince (*Chaenomeles* x *superba* 'Nicoline')
Rose (*Rosa* 'Danse du Feu'; R. 'Guinée')
Lion's ear (*Leonotis leonurus*)

YELLOW

Day lily (*Hemerocallis*)
Primrose (*Primula vulgaris*)
Yarrow (*Achillea filipendulina* 'Gold Plate')
Sunflower (*Helianthus*)
Clematis (*Clematis tangutica*)
Rose (*Rosa* 'Golden Showers')
Coronilla valentina subsp. *glauca*
Forsythia x *intermedia* 'Spectabilis'
Lady's mantle (*Alchemilla mollis*)
Peony (*Paeonia mlokosewitschii*)

BLUE

Love-in-the-mist (*Nigella damascena* 'Miss Jekyll')
Anemone (*Anemone nemorosa* 'Atrocaerulea')
Hardy geranium (*Geranium* 'Johnson's Blue')
Iris reticulata
Forget-me-not (*Myosotis*)
Spring gentian (*Gentiana verna*)
Hyssop (*Hyssopus officinalis*)
California lilac (*Ceanothus impressus*)
Hibiscus (*Hibiscus syriacus* 'Oiseau Bleu')

MAUVE AND PURPLE

Lilac (*Syringa* x *hyacinthiflora* 'Esther Staley')
Clematis 'Jackmanii'; *C.* 'Vyvyan Pennell'
Mourning widow (*Geranium phaeum* var. *phaeum*)
Christmas rose (*Helleborus atrorubens*)
Butterfly bush (*Buddleja davidii* 'Black Knight')
Sweet violet (*Viola odorata*)
Hebe 'Alicia Amherst'
Lavender (*Lavandula angustifolia* 'Hidcote')
Rose (*Rosa* 'Cardinal de Richelieu'; *R.* 'Roseraie de l'Haÿ')

WHITE

Rose (*Rosa* 'Mme Hardy'; *R.* 'Mme Alfred Carrière'; *R.* 'Iceberg')
Lilac (*Syringa* 'Mme Lemoine')
Snowdrop (*Galanthus nivalis*)
Bleeding heart (*Dicentra formosa alba*)
Orange blossom (*Philadelphus* 'Manteau d'Hermine')
Viburnum x *carlcephalum*
Mexican orange blossom (*Choisya ternata*)
Solomon's seal (*Polygonatum* x *hybridum*)
Old-fashioned pink (*Dianthus* 'Mrs Sinkins')
Foxglove (*Digitalis purpurea* f. *albiflora*)
Hosta sieboldii var. *alba*

interior design with colour

Have you ever felt uncomfortable in a room without knowing why? It may have had something to do with the colours in which it was decorated. This has no connection with fashion; it is simply about choosing the most suitable colours for a particular room.

Very often, we learn about this the hard way. Someone might decorate her living room walls with a lovely, bright red wallpaper. At night with the lights on, it looks cosy but it might be very difficult to relax in it or the family could keep having silly disagreements and arguments, without knowing why. Someone else might choose a sharp, slightly acid, yellow-green for the walls in her big kitchen. She might be the best cook in the world but people may not be very enthusiastic about her food when they eat in her kitchen. It has nothing to do with her cooking – the fault lies with the yellow-green walls, which create a slight sense of nausea.

This doesn't mean you can never use red in your living room or yellow in your kitchen. Instead, you must be careful about the shade you use, and the amount of it.

An intense blue like this is very relaxing, provided that you can balance it with a neutral colour, otherwise it will become oppressive and depressing.

consider the room's purpose

The first step is to consider what you will be doing in a particular room. The main colours must be appropriate for that activity. Put simply, you want restful colours for rooms in which you will be resting, stimulating colours for rooms in which you will be active, and so on. It also makes sense to choose colours that you like, and which the rest of the household likes as well. Happily, there are thousands of shades, tints and tones of colours, so you are bound to find something you like.

the kitchen

This room is the place where we prepare and eat our food, so it's a good idea to decorate it in colours that are clean and stimulating. If you want your friends and family to congregate around your kitchen table, relaxing and enjoying themselves, choose colours that are welcoming and comforting but aren't so stimulating that they make everyone restless, argumentative and unable to sit still. Look for warm oranges, terracottas and pinky-reds. Add splashes of rich yellow to encourage lively conversation. Alternatively, if you want a kitchen with a very clean atmosphere, you might like to choose a neutral tint. You can always add colour with bowls, storage containers and other accessories.

the living room

Once again, you must consider the atmosphere that you want to create in your living room and the sort of activities that will take place there. Is it a room designed specifically for relaxing and watching television? If so, you need restful, relaxing colours that will help you to switch off from the concerns of the day. Light greens and pale pinks are welcoming yet calming. On the other hand, if you do a lot of entertaining or if this room is the main meeting place of the household, you might prefer to choose gently stimulating colours that will encourage everyone to mingle and chat. Look for orangey-yellow colours such as peach and coral.

know your colour terminology

Colours are divided into tints, tones and shades, which are defined below:

Tints *Colours to which white has been added.*

Tones *Colours to which grey has been added.*

Shades *Colours to which black has been added.*

The immediate impression of this room is one of calm. This is created by the light green of the sofa and the neutral walls. Too bare a room, however, can seem unfriendly.

The restful colour scheme of amethyst and white in a bedroom fosters a peaceful atmosphere which is conducive to a good night's sleep.

the bedroom

When choosing the colours for your bedroom, you must consider what you'll be doing in it. Do you want it to be a seductive, romantic space? Or a peaceful oasis of calm? Such considerations are especially important if you're a light sleeper, because you must choose colours that will help you to sleep well.

Avoid too much yellow because its ability to stimulate the mind may mean that you spend a lot of time lying awake at night, with endless thoughts flying through your head. Red, even though it can create a sensual, warm atmosphere, which is perfect for sharing with a partner, can be overpowering when used in too great a quantity. Instead of dropping off into a restful sleep, you are more likely to feel tense and possibly even claustrophobic. Try to introduce red through lampshades, throws and curtains, and avoid sleeping on red sheets or pillows because you'll feel restless and could wake up boiling hot in the middle of the night. Light pink is a good compromise, as it creates a safe, loving atmosphere.

Blue is one of the most suitable colours for a bedroom because it's such a restful colour. However, you might prefer to choose touches of a warm blue, such as cobalt or cerulean, rather than a very cold blue, especially if the room is chilly. Even if you don't want to paint the walls blue, consider using it for your bedding. Going to sleep on a blue pillowcase will be a much more restful experience than if you choose a brightly patterned fabric. This is especially important if you are a light sleeper or are prone to insomnia.

White always looks clean in a bathroom, whereas too much white can create a clinical atmosphere in the other rooms of the house.

the bathroom

Do you want a sensual, hedonistic bathroom where you retreat for long pampering sessions, or would you prefer a bathroom that always looks clean and hygienic? If you're opting for the clean look, blue and white is a highly effective combination. Introduce silver in the form of sparkling chrome bathroom fittings. For a more sybaritic experience, you could use warm pinks and turquoises, which are relaxing.

the study or home office

If you work from home you may want to convert one of the rooms in your home into a study or office. As ever, you should consider the atmosphere that you want to create before choosing the decorations. If your work involves plenty of thought and mental agility, you should introduce touches of yellow to the room. Too much of it, though, will make it hard for you to concentrate, and if all the walls are yellow it can be counter-productive. If your work involves self-expression, your office should incorporate blue and orange. If you work as a healer or complementary health therapist, you could add touches of violet and amethyst.

wearing colour

Have you ever put on an item of clothing and then taken it off immediately because the colour felt wrong? If so, you're already working with colour in your life. There are some days when a particular colour is too strong or too weak for us, when we feel drab in it or overpowered by it. Whenever this happens to you, it's worth paying attention to the colour you've rejected and the colour you've chosen in its place, and thinking about what this says about your mood at that time.

The colours you choose to wear say a tremendous amount about you, regardless of what happens to be at the height of fashion. Unless you are a total slave to the latest fashions and completely change your wardrobe each season, or you only dress in one particular colour (never a good idea, as it will unbalance you), you will wear a range of colours.

paint it black

For many years now, black has been the fail-safe fashion colour. You only have to think of Audrey Hepburn in her classic, black Givenchy dress in *Breakfast at Tiffany's* to know how chic black can look. In the right outfit, black can make a very sophisticated statement. However, it can also help you to fade into the background. It's a colour that withdraws and hides. It's often the first choice for people who are feeling insecure or possibly even depressed.

As a colour, black absorbs light. It can therefore absorb the energies around it, which means it can soak up negative emotions. This means you should always offset black with another colour, even if it isn't visible. If you want to wear black from head to toe, make sure you're wearing some brightly coloured underwear.

wardrobe analysis

1 Choose a time when you won't be disturbed and you can take your time over this exercise. Look in your wardrobe or drawers to see which are the prevailing colours. Try to look at them objectively, as though they belong to someone else. Don't make any judgements about your clothes.

2 Listen to your gut instincts as you look at the colours of your clothes. Is there an emphasis on one or more colours? If so, which ones are they? Based on your knowledge of colour, what are the psychological associations of these colours?

3 Now pull out an item of clothing that you rarely wear. Most of us have at least one of these! Look at its colour or colours. Do the colours explain why you never wear this piece of clothing? Put it on and look at yourself in the mirror. How do you feel now?

4 Now turn to one of your favourite pieces of clothing. Objectively note the colour and what this says about you. Is it the same colour as the rejected piece of clothing? If so, do you now know why you wear one but not the other?

5 Finally, consider whether you are now ready to try wearing different colours or if you're still happy with your current choice of colour.

An all-black outfit may look chic but it can have a negative impact on our emotions. Black clothes should be balanced by coloured underwear, or vice versa.

Earthy colours, such as browns and sage greens, help us to connect with nature and therefore have a grounding effect on our emotions.

when to wear ...

Each colour has a particular energy from which you can benefit. So when you're undecided about what to wear for a forthcoming event or to trigger a particular mood, use this guide to give you some ideas.

RED

This dynamic colour can help to lift your spirits, making you feel energized, bold and assertive. Even a few splashes of red will increase your confidence. It's a colour to wear when you want to be noticed and when you're happy for people to look at you. Red socks or shoes will help to ground you, especially if you're feeling light-headed or you're living too much in your mind. Red is also an excellent choice on cold days, because it's such a warming colour.

PINK

One of the colours of unconditional love, pink is a good choice when you want to be more loving and kind. It helps to defuse difficult situations, so is a good choice if you want to avoid losing your temper.

ORANGE

Less powerful than red, orange is a great colour to wear when you want to boost your optimism and creativity, and feel more in control of your life. It's a carefree colour, so too much of it may not be appropriate for very formal occasions. Orange is a particularly good choice when you want to assert your individuality, have the courage to be your true self and also to embrace change. It's a very sociable and cheering colour, so it's perfect if you're going to a party and you want to attract people to you without being the centre of attention.

YELLOW

This is the colour to wear if you want to create order in your life. It's an excellent choice when you want to clarify your thoughts, such as when attending an important meeting, trying to make a decision or sitting an exam.

GREEN

Green is the great balancer, so is a good choice when you want to see both sides of a story or you simply want to create harmony around you. This is also one of the two colours of unconditional love, helping you to accept others as they truly are. It's a restful, soothing colour, and its associations with nature help to foster a sense of calm and also of being connected with the universe. It's a good choice if you've been under a lot of stress, and also if you're resisting change because it will give you the courage to move on. Acid greens give you an energy boost.

BLUE

This is a restful, peaceful and soothing colour, so it's helpful when you're going through a crisis or life is very hectic. Blue will help you to slow down and relax. Therefore, it's a great choice for clothes in which to meditate or sleep. Above all, though, blue is the colour of communication so it's an ideal choice when you want to express your ideas and listen to those of others.

If you're sensitive to colour, you will have days when you can wear a particular shade and others when you don't feel right in it at all.

colour for babies and children

Babies' clothes have come a long way since they were uniformly dressed in pale pastels, such as creams, pale lemons, pinks and blues. Today, babies wear much brighter colours, including clear reds and greens. However, although these might look very nice, such colours don't always do the babies much good.

The fact is, young babies need gentle, pastel colours. Strong primaries are far too powerful for them, because babies under nine months old are spiritually still in transition from the spirit realms to their current incarnation. Gentle pinks, pale corals and soft oranges – whether for a girl or a boy – are all suitable colours because they are reminiscent of the safety and warmth of the mother's womb. White is also an excellent choice because it contains all the colours of the spectrum, thereby allowing the child to connect with and absorb the colours he needs.

Very young babies get cold easily, so their heads are often covered. Once again, you should be careful about the colours that you choose for a baby's bonnet, because his crown chakra is still wide open so will quickly absorb the energy of the colours that cover it. Bright reds and blues, vibrant yellows and hot pinks will all agitate the child, possibly even leading to restlessness and an inability to settle whenever he's put down for a sleep. If the child has cradle cap, which is an inflammation of the scalp common to many babies, these hot colours

Bright colours for very small babies may be fashionable and look cheery but they are far too strong for them. Old-fashioned pastel shades are much more appropriate.

might even make it worse. You can help to alleviate the condition by giving the baby a violet hat or bonnet.

Pay attention to the colour of your baby's bedclothes, too. Choose white, soft pinks or amethyst to create a calm atmosphere and lull your baby off to sleep. The colours of the bedding will penetrate your child's aura, so they should be gentle and soothing.

children's bedrooms

When a child is older you can safely start introducing him to every colour of the spectrum. Encourage your child to play with toys of different colours so he can gain a greater understanding of them.

Even so, you should still be careful about the colours you use to decorate your child's bedroom. Keep bright, invigorating colours such as reds and oranges away from your child's bed, to encourage restful sleep at night. This includes large toys, bean bags and other items. Duvet covers decorated with images of your child's favourite cartoon character may be good fun and encourage him to scramble into bed each night, but if the design is very hectic it will interfere with his sleep patterns. Such fabrics are best confined to the curtains and other soft furnishings, provided that they're well away from the bed.

As your child gets older, he will need an area in which to study and do his homework. Ideally, you should set aside a part of his bedroom that's well away from his bed, to keep his working and sleeping areas separate. Decorate the study area of his room with yellows, to stimulate his mind and keep his ideas fresh. You could balance this yellow with touches of indigo or violet, to reduce the vibrancy of the yellow and create a calmer atmosphere. If this is impractical, give your child yellow-covered files and notebooks, and yellow pencils, or put a yellow painting or poster on the wall above his desk.

The yellows in this nursery boost creativity but they are balanced perfectly by the violets, creating a calm, restful atmosphere for sleep.

colour healing through diet

One of the best and easiest ways to apply colour healing is through the food we eat. It's long been said that we eat with our eyes first, and therefore we're more likely to enjoy food that looks colourful than food that looks bland and uninteresting. Years ago, a typical meal for an invalid was all white: steamed white fish, mashed potato and cauliflower, followed by a milk pudding. It may have been easy to digest but it was hardly a feast for the eyes!

For a well-balanced diet, we should aim to eat as many different coloured foods in each meal as possible. The fresher they are, the better they are for us.

Nature has made sure that food comes in a stunning array of colours. In fact, each type of food we eat belongs to one of the seven colours of the rainbow. Therefore, if you want to increase the amount of exposure you have to a particular colour, you can do so by increasing the amount of food that you eat of that colour. However, you must always balance it with its complementary colour.

eating well

In recent years, there has been massive interest in nutrition and the importance of the food that we eat, which has neatly coincided with the ever-increasing variety of food that is available to buy. Yet, ironically, it seems that fewer people are learning to cook properly and obesity rates are ballooning.

One of the best ways you can keep healthy is to eat a balanced diet, and to have as much variety in it as possible. This not only means eating a wide selection of fruit and vegetables, grains, pulses, dairy products, animal and/or vegetable proteins and fats, but also many different herbs and spices. In China, it's considered essential to eat at least 30 different foods each day (which includes spices). In the West, some people don't even manage to eat 30 different foods in a week because their diets are so restricted and unimaginative.

The pink of this fruit smoothie tells us that it is full of energy that will quickly be absorbed by our bodies.

a colourful diet

Once you've started to learn about the impact that colour has on your life, you'll instinctively begin to pay more attention to the colour of what's on your plate. Your sensitivity to colour will be enhanced, and as a result you'll become more aware of the effects that different coloured foods have on you. There may be days, for instance, when all you long for are red foods, and others when you don't want them at all. Always trust your intuition with this, because then you'll know what your body needs.

other considerations

In addition to your increased sensitivity to the colours of the foods you're eating, you may find that you become more sensitive to other dietary factors as well. You might be drawn to organic or biodynamic foods rather than those sprayed with pesticides and preservatives. If you normally eat meat or fish, you might start to reduce your intake of them because you find that they lower your body's vibrations or you're concerned about the way the animal was killed. Any food allergies that you have might become more apparent or you may realize that you're becoming increasingly sensitive to refined sugar and starches. Let this process happen naturally, and don't resist it. It's an important way for your body to talk to you.

the rainbow on your plate

If you'd like to extend colour healing to your diet, the following pages will give you some guidelines to consider and guidance about the different colour groups to which some foods belong. Before you read them, jot down a list of your favourite foods, especially those that make you feel good when you eat them. Write them down without consciously thinking about their colours, and then review the list. You might find that your favourite foods all belong to one or two specific colour groups.

If you realize that you rarely eat foods from a particular colour group, make a conscious effort to start doing so because it means you're missing out on some vital foods. You might also find that the missing colour corresponds to a health problem. For instance, you may realize that you often get migraines yet you never eat the blue foods that could help to alleviate the condition.

The rise of organic vegetable box schemes and farmers' markets helps us to eat foods that have been grown locally in season, and which are therefore fresher and still full of nutrients.

fresh is best

Regardless of how you structure your diet or introduce new foods into it, always try to eat your food when it's as fresh as possible. This ensures that it has plenty of vitality and energy, which you in turn will absorb. If it's difficult to buy fresh vegetables, consider buying them frozen instead because they'll have been frozen shortly after picking. Fruit and vegetables that are old and flabby are barely worth eating, other than for their fibre content, because they've lost all their goodness. However, it's a different story when they're freshly picked because you can still sense their life force. Once you've eaten an apple straight from the tree or a tomato that's still warm from the Sun, you'll know the difference between 'dead' food and 'alive' food.

table matters

Do you pay any attention to the colour of the cups and plates you use? As you become more attuned to colour, you'll realize that it's nicer to use some plates than others. You'll find it hard to relax and enjoy your food if you're eating it off a red plate, because you'll be in a rush. You might even get indigestion soon after finishing your meal. Food eaten from a yellow plate may make you feel slightly nauseous, especially if it was fatty food.

Coloured china may look attractive but it can have unwitting effects on our mood and appetite. White or cream china does not do this.

some important guidelines

Before you begin to extend colour healing to your diet, there are some important facts that you need to know.

* Foods for colour healing are classified by their outer colour as well as by the action that they have on our bodies, so you may find some foods listed in two different categories. For instance, foods that supply a lot of energy are classified as red foods, even if they aren't coloured red.

* It is important to balance the colours you're using. For instance, you shouldn't embark on a single-colour diet because that will create an imbalance in your body. Do your best to choose foods for each meal that belong to complementary colours, so their energies are balanced. For instance, you might want a yellow and purple meal.

* Foods in your favourite colours supply the energy and nutrients that your body needs most of all.

* Foods in the colours that you like least supply the energy and nutrients that your body is lacking.

* Green is the colour of balance, so always try to eat something from this category at every meal. If you suspect that your diet contains too much or too little of a particular colour, green food will help to counteract this (unless you're already only eating green food).

Raspberries are one of the delicious soft fruits. Ideally, for the greatest nutritional benefit, they should be eaten in season.

red foods

Red foods have a vibrant, energizing effect on the body. They help to enrich our red blood cells, so can be helpful in cases of anaemia. They provide energy that is used rapidly by the body, and they also help to ground us. Iron-rich foods belong in this category.

Red vegetables Tomatoes, red peppers, radishes, red potatoes, chillies, watercress, leafy dark green vegetables such as spinach and ruby chard

Red fruit Red apples, red grapes, rhubarb, cherries, cherry plums, plums, tayberries, pomegranates, strawberries, raspberries, loganberries, cranberries, mulberries, watermelon, redcurrants

Red pulses, grains, seeds and nuts Red kidney beans, aduki beans, borlotti beans, pinto beans, red rice

Red foods from animals and fish Red meat, offal, red snapper

Red herbs and spices Cloves, cinnamon, cayenne pepper, paprika

orange foods

Orange foods have a warming and stimulating impact on the body but aren't as powerful as red foods. They can therefore be a good substitute for red foods if these aren't suitable. Orange foods help to increase our creativity, enthusiasm and optimism. They also act as a tonic and help to rid the body of toxins.

Orange vegetables Carrots, orange peppers, orange chillies, squash, pumpkin, swede

Orange fruit Oranges, clementines, peaches, nectarines, papaya, physalis, cantaloupe melon, mangoes, guavas, apricots

Orange pulses, grains, seeds and nuts Split red lentils, baked beans, buckwheat, peanut butter, walnuts

Orange foods from animals and fish Egg yolks, poultry, salmon, smoked salmon, prawns, scallops

Orange herbs and spices Nutmeg, coriander, cumin, ginger, marigold petals, nasturtium petals

Butternut squash is a very versatile vegetable and for cooking purposes can be treated in exactly the same way as potatoes.

yellow foods

These foods increase our mental abilities, encourage concentration, generally boost the thought processes and combat the tendency to worry. In addition to the foods listed below, any food grown in full sunlight will have yellow properties.

Yellow vegetables Onions, potatoes, parsnips, sweetcorn, yellow peppers, squash, salsify

Yellow fruit Bananas, pears, lemons, grapefruit, pineapples

Yellow pulses, grains, seeds and nuts Butter beans, chickpeas, yellow split peas, rice, pasta, couscous, quinoa, bulgar wheat, oats, sesame seeds, sunflower seeds, Brazil nuts, cashew nuts, almonds

Sage is an invaluable herb that can be grown in a pot on a windowsill or outdoors. You can use it fresh or dried.

Yellow foods from animals and fish Poultry, honey, butter, cheese, haddock, kippers

Yellow herbs and spices Turmeric, saffron, lemon thyme, caraway seeds, yellow mustard seeds

green foods

Green foods have a calming effect on the body and emotions. They can also help to reduce blood pressure, strengthen the heart and reduce stress. Always try to eat some green food at each meal, because it will help to balance the energy of the other colours that you're eating.

Green vegetables Lettuce, watercress, kale, spinach, cabbage, broccoli, cauliflower, celery, leeks, Brussels sprouts, cucumbers, avocados, courgettes, artichokes, peas, beans, spring onions, fennel, okra, green olives

Green fruit Limes, kiwifruit, green grapes, greengages, gooseberries, Ogen melons, apples

Green pulses, grains, seeds and nuts Green lentils, mung beans, olive oil, pumpkin seeds

Green foods from animals and fish White fish, milk, yogurt

Green herbs and spices Chives, basil, coriander, parsley, mint, bay leaves, marjoram, oregano, sage

blue, indigo and violet foods

These three colour categories have been grouped together because there are fewer of them. They all help to balance the heat and warmth of red, orange and yellow foods. Foods in these colours help to combat stress and tension, and are especially beneficial when life is very hectic and it's difficult to relax and take time out. They encourage contemplation and restfulness. Of all the colour categories, this is the one that we often forget, so ensure that you eat plenty of these foods.

Oily fish, such as mackerel, belongs to the blue and indigo categories of food.

Blue, indigo and violet vegetables
Aubergines, purple peppers, red onions, purple sprouting broccoli, beetroot, red cabbage, seaweed, asparagus, mushrooms, black olives, garlic, purple kohlrabi

Blue, indigo and violet fruit Blueberries, bilberries, blackberries, blackcurrants, black cherries, plums, damsons, figs, dates, prunes, raisins, currants, mulberries, dessert gooseberries

Blue, indigo and violet pulses, grains, seeds and nuts Puy lentils, black beans, black mustard seeds, pistachio nuts

Blue, indigo and violet foods from animals and fish Shellfish, sardines, mackerel

Blue, indigo and violet herbs and spices Purple sage, purple basil, rosemary, licorice root, soy sauce

index

acknowledgements

Alamy/ Bubbles Photolibrary 116; /Chad Ehlers 105; /Elizabeth Whiting & Associates 117; /IndustrialPhoto 32; /Ken Weingart 28; /The Print Collector 15; /Westend61 51. **Corbis UK Ltd**/Abode Beateworks 24; /Bettmann 10; /ImageShop 26; /Jon Feingersh/zefa 55; /Jose Luis Pelaez, Inc. 118; /Tim Pannell 109. **Getty Images**/Image Source Black 25; /Inti St. Clair 108; /Justin Pumfrey 61; /Photolibrary 113; /redcover.com 110; /Ricky John Molloy 33; /Robbert Koene 111; /Siri Stafford 41; /Thomas Barwick 40; /Time & Life Pictures 12. **istockphoto.com**/Stuart Pitkin 121. **Octopus Publishing Group Limited** 39, 70, 70, 97; /David Loftus 30; /David Sarton 107; /Davis Sarton 103; /Frank Adam 122, 125; /Lis Parsons 119, 123; /Mike Prior 115; /Ruth Jenkinson 65, 69; /Steve Gorton 38; /Vanessa Davies 114; /William Reavell 124. **Photolibrary**/Kim Steele 57. **PhotoDisc** 16. **Science & Society Picture Library**/Science Museum 94. **Science Photo Library**/Annabella Bluesky 95; /Lawrence Lawry 13; /Seymour 11 bottom. **Shutterstock**/Dimitry Kosterev 37; /Elena Elisseeva 104; /Giangrande Alessia 11; /Shawn Zhang 29; /Stavchansky Yakov 35. /Tomas Loutocky 102.

Pages 20–21 courtesy of Picture of Inner Light Workers www.innerlightworkers.co.uk. Content © Hilary Hargreaves, School of Inner Light www.schoolofinnerlight.co.uk. Artist Hilary Stanley www.amethystbourne.co.uk.

Executive editor: Sandra Rigby
Editor: Camilla Davis
Executive art editor: Penny Stock
Designer: Barbara Zuñiga
Photographer: Russell Sadur
Picture library assistant Taura Riley
Senion production controller: Simone Nauerth